Successful Asso

Dimensions of 21st-Century Competency for the CEO

by Glenn Tecker and Marybeth Fidler

ISBN 0-88034-073-8

The Foundation of the American Society
    of Association Executives
1575 Eye Street, N.W.
Washington, DC 20005-1168

Printed in the United States of America

This book is dedicated to Richard MacAdoo—our friend, partner, and colleague. His insightful contributions to the project, his professional family, and the field of association management have left all immeasurably better. Richard's wisdom, commitment, and caring counsel are profoundly missed by many.

About the Authors

Glenn Tecker is President and Chief Executive Officer of Tecker Consultants, an international consulting firm specializing in management, education, and organization. Glenn has served as an association executive and as a board member for both non-profit and for-profit organizations. His other published works with ASAE include *Assessing Your Strengths and Weaknesses* and the *Association Education Handbook*.

Marybeth Fidler is senior partner with Tecker Consultants and principal, Marybeth Fidler, Consultant. Fidler is immediate past executive director of a 190,000 member international association, and former chief elected officer of a 30,000 member professional association. She completed her fourteen year banking career in 1987, declining two bank CEO positions in favor of association management and consulting. A published poet and abstract acrylic artist, Fidler resides in Long Beach, California.

Foreword

The ASAE Foundation has addressed the needs of associations and their executives since its inception in 1963, resulting in a broad array of research studies and publications. In 1989, the Foundation studied leadership issues from an organizational perspective in *Leading the Association: Striking the Right Balance between Staff and Volunteers*. We have now extended this inquiry into the realm of personal leadership with Tecker Consultants' study of executive competencies for the 21st century.

The demographic, economic, and social trends of the past few decades have resulted in association executives' need for a new array of skills and behaviors—new competencies. This study draws on extensive confidential interviews and the review of more than 600 case study files to identify those competencies now most critical to the current and future success of association executives.

Additionally, recent studies suggest a perception that many association executives spend far too much effort attempting to impress their peers rather than attempting to impress their members with improving products and services. This study discusses this and similar phenomena and describes actions executives must take to avoid becoming a career-change statistic.

The ASAE Foundation Board of Directors is indebted to those organizations and individuals listed on the following page whose generous support has made this research possible. We are deeply appreciative of their leadership role in this effort.

Special thanks are due to Lee VanBremen, Ph.D., CAE, executive vice president of the College of American Pathologists, for his dual leadership roles in seeking support for this study and for overseeing its development.

This book provides guidance for association executives in understanding the key competencies of 21st-century association executives and how to change their lives if necessary to succeed. The self-diagnostic tools included will help executives in this change and will identify areas for continued professional growth and development. We trust this important addition to the body of knowledge of association management will be of practical value to today's and tomorrow's association executives as we lead our organizations into the 21st century.

Garis F. Distelhorst, CAE
Chief Staff Executive, National Association of College Stores
1992–93 Chair, ASAE Foundation

The Board of Directors of the ASAE Foundation wish to acknowledge the generous contributions of the following organizations and individuals, whose support made this study possible:

President's Counselors
National Association of College Stores
National Association of Realtors
Tau Kappa Epsilon International Fraternity
Technical Association of the Pulp and Paper Industry

Ambassadors
American Academy of Orthopaedic Surgeons
American Association of Museums
American Association of Orthodontists
American College of Emergency Physicians—National Office
American Industrial Hygiene Association
California Medical Association
Hyatt Hotels Corporation
Printing Industries of America

Envoys
American Booksellers Association Incorporated
American Hotel and Motel Association
Anaheim Convention and Visitors Bureau
National Association of Professional Insurance Agents
Robert L. Olcott, CAE
Produce Marketing Association
Shearson Lehman Brothers

Diplomats
International Association of Refrigerated Warehouses
Seattle King County Convention and Visitors Bureau

Acknowledgments

We are deeply appreciative of the efforts of the many whose contributions, candor, and enthusiasm have made this project a reality. The Foundation of the American Society of Association Executives made this project possible by providing funding and editorial guidance through its completion. Thank you to the Foundation Board, and its committed and energetic staff. A special thank you is extended to Garis Distelhorst, 1992–93 Foundation Chair, who, two years before he knew he would assume the chair, sought a proposal for this book after hearing about its antecedent study at a committee meeting.

This project was also heavily dependent on the contributions of the Tecker Consultants' research team: Cate Bower, Don Calderon, Bud Crouch, Kermit Eide, Larry Garfield, Richard McAdoo, and Steve Michaele. Their contributions of insights, experiences, and efforts in delineating the competencies has been invaluable to the completion of this project. A special thanks to Cate Bower who prepared the initial draft of Chapter 3, and the tireless staff at Tecker Consultants for their support in preparation of the final draft.

And perhaps most important, we wish to acknowledge the support and candid feedback received from hundreds of chief staff officers from across North America and especially the executives, who were interviewed in depth, who helped us to refine and validate the research results. We regret that our commitment to anonymity prevents acknowledgment by name, but this in no way diminishes the heartfelt gratitude we extend to this key group of contributors.

As association consulting professionals, we have a commitment to contributing to the health and vitality of the association industry. It is our hope that in some small measure this study will illuminate the path that we all seek toward a future of excellence in fulfilling member needs.

Glenn Tecker   Marybeth Fidler

Table of Contents

List of Exhibits

SECTION I

The Context:
Why These Competencies?

CHAPTER 1
The Purpose of the Study

The future viability of every association is either threatened or encouraged by a growing number of fundamental demographic, business, and societal trends. Consequently, the competencies required by many association executives will change in response to the shifting roles and dynamics of the associations they serve, and the nature and composition of their elected and volunteer leadership.

Today, association executives already spend the vast majority of their time managing two interrelated areas: relationships and information. Expert analysis, based on research into case study files, strongly suggests that:

- Failures in these two essential areas are the primary reasons for association executive terminations; successful execution of competencies in these two areas is the common characteristic of successful executives.
- The specific competencies in these two areas of association management are poorly defined and seldom or ineffectively addressed in executive educational initiatives.
- Many executives are broadly aware of some of these competencies and are able to discuss them, but they are unable or ineffective in the actual execution of appropriate behaviors in real situations.

- **Competency in these two areas will be the key to success for 21st-century association executives.**

We have also noticed that many top association positions are being awarded to people from outside the profession of association management. Some observers feel many association executives have created a world for themselves that is now out of touch with the needs and expectations of the very people they serve. They suggest that too many of today's association executives may:

- be functionally knowledgeable, but behaviorally incompetent;
- not understand the difference between manipulation and leadership;
- be more concerned with the role of executive and the nature of the position than they are with doing a good job for those they are supposed to be serving; or
- be trying to grow the association beyond what the members want or need it to be.

Whether this is true or not, we believe the fact that these perceptions exist is significant. Combining this with the volatility of the environment, association executives are beginning to question not only the future nature and role of trade associations and individual membership societies, but of the association executive as well. Questions are being asked, such as:

- "Will my organization be around in the year 2000, and if so, what will it look like?"
- "Will I be around as an association executive in the year 2000?"
- "Are the skills and behaviors of today's association executive appropriate for tomorrow's association?"
- "How can I maintain the competencies, confidence, and creativity so important to success?"
- "Have we built a house in which we cannot live?"

The answers to these questions and the articulation of competencies important to 21st-century association leaders are essential information for both staff and volunteer leadership. The destabilizing impact of executive turnover on an association is significant. Organizational energy is redirected to replacement activity, strategic momentum is interrupted, and staff productivity is affected. When a stable environment is present, it is a generally accepted premise that the presence of a highly competent and effective association executive is one of the primary keys to organizational achievement and success.

Purpose and Contribution

The purpose of this study and the resulting book has been to delineate the critical competency issues relevant to associations and their executives into, and beyond, the year 2000.

We hope that by using the insights provided, association executives will be better able to understand the changing environment in which we all operate, and recognize areas in their own professional and personal lives that can be expanded and shifted to promote continued success in the profession. The adage "forewarned is forearmed" comes to mind as one real purpose for this book. If association executives recognize ahead of time the direction and speed of many of the changes unfolding in the field, then they will be better prepared to adjust to them and take advantage of a new kind of emerging opportunity for contribution. It is our hope that the ultimate result of this study will be that associations, and the staff executives partnered with members in leading them, will transcend issues of survival, and prosper as successful societal and business leaders well beyond the year 2000.

Study Design

The competency study completed under the auspices of the Foundation of the American Society of Association Executives was designed to accomplish the following:

- Identify the essential competencies of 21st-century executives by expert analysis of over 600 case study files of Tecker Consultant's engagements with associations, societies, foundations, other types of not-for-profit organizations, and for-profit associations or subsidiaries.
- Respect the anonymity of individuals and associations represented in the study population by carefully and steadfastly protecting their identities at all times. All research sources, materials, and analysis session records will remain confidential.
- Define the executive competencies of the future and their attendant behaviors by developing parallel behavioral sets, descriptions of successful execution of competencies, the absence of competencies, and/or the ineffective execution of the competencies.
- Link these essential competencies to trends and paradigm shifts occurring within the association arena.
- Validate the resulting competencies with highly effective association executives within the not-for-profit sector.

Overview

In the early chapters of this book we provide a context description of the environment in which association executives and leaders find themselves operating. Chapter 2 is focused on the special nature of associations because the dynamics of not-for-profit organizations creates a working environment that makes these competencies especially essential for association leaders. What are the common elements of associations relevant to appreciating the importance of these competencies? What are the stages in the life cycle of an association and the implications of each stage for the effective execution of leadership?

Chapter 3 is designed to be a snapshot of current and evolving conditions. Why is it that good executives get fired? What causes the moment of truth when the partnership between a good chief staff executive and a board of directors becomes apparently unreconcilable?

Chapter 4 is a look at the major, common trends affecting associations today and the implications of these trends for fundamental shifts in the paradigm of many associations. These trends include the changing nature of change itself, increased demand for outcome accountability, less time from volunteers, technology, and generational and multicultural diversity.

Finally, Chapters 5 through 10 articulate the competencies that will be increasingly critical for association executives as the nature and organizational condition of associations evolve into the 21st century.

An appendix provides two self-appraisal questionnaires for readers interested in conducting a snapshot perceptual assessment of the (a) condition of their own "professional competence"; and/or (b) the condition of their association's "organizational health."

CHAPTER 2
The Special Nature of Associations

Not-for-profit associations as formal, complex, and legally sanctioned enterprises are a relatively new institutional form in organizational history. Not prevalent prior to the 20th century, such organizations represent a young and still changing phenomena in the evolution of organized groups. They are growing rapidly in numbers, size, diversity, and impact.

Associations are created when a group of like-minded individuals decide to join together to transform or shape the world in which they live, rather than allow their world to be shaped for them by others. Whether the group's motivation is to shape the regulatory or business environment, to raise public awareness, or to empower its members to be more effective in their world, the fundamental value shared by all associations is that groups of people actively working together will be more effective in bringing about change than will individual efforts operating in isolation.

Though associations vary greatly in their size, scope, and mission, there are commonalities in the basic nature of such organizations which can provide us with significant understanding of the sometimes peculiar dynamics of association management and leadership. We begin by offering a basic definition of an association:

Association: A group of people who voluntarily come together to meet common needs, solve common problems, and accomplish common goals.

Several elements of this definition present significant and unique challenges for managers and leaders of associations.

Groups of People

One thing that can be said with great certainty about groups of people is that they are unpredictable. (Some would even go so far as to say fickle!) If you find this notion disconcerting, consider this example: How often has an association leadership which believes it has constructed a portfolio of programs, services, and products designed to be attractive to the broad diversity of its membership, been surprised by a significant segment of members with their own "targeted" agenda.

Though frustrating to leadership, the reasons for such common occurrences are simple. *The opinions people have, the judgments they make, and the decisions they reach are in large measure premised on the perceptions they have.* These perceptions do not always match reality because our perceptions are based on the information that we have available. Therein lies a basic and critical insight for successful association leaders. They recognize that by virtue of their role in the organization, they have access to relevant information that is broader, deeper, and more frequently updated than the information available to the vast majority of the membership. For that reason, they understand that the leader's view of the world can often be significantly different than the view of the world held by the majority of the members. They appreciate that this does not mean one view is better or worse than the other. But it does mean that the views of leaders and members will be different. This situation is especially true for issues that have to do with the future. Thinking about the future involves judgments about what must be done today to prepare for the tomorrow being sought. A leader's view of what is and what is to come will be dramatically affected by exposure to the broad thinking, accurate information, and insightful ideas to which members do not have frequent access.

Information—The Leadership Role

This understanding leads to recognition of two fundamental obligations of association leadership. Both of these obligations have to do with information. Because the effective use of information is a theme throughout 21st-century competencies, these two obligations are especially relevant to the focus of this study.

First, today's associations are, for the most part, in the information business—collecting, managing, distributing, or creating access to information in one way or another. Many associations today are also in, or preparing to enter, the knowledge business. This means transforming raw data and descriptive information by including interpretation, advice, and judgment about what on an increasingly extensive list of things to know is most important to pay attention to, and how that information can be specifically applied by the user. In today's world, members are faced with an overwhelming amount of information from which to draw to manage complex businesses, professions, or lives. The transformation of information into knowledge is rapidly becoming a critical service, benefit, and demand of members. This dynamic is already affecting the business lines and organizational cultures of many associations. It significantly impacts on the nature of the organization in which leadership will be provided in the 21st century.

Whether an association is in the information or knowledge business, leadership obligation is the same—to access a continual stream of information from members that allows the leader to remain sensitive to and aware of member needs, expectations, problems, and desires. Not what the leader thinks they ought to be, but what, in fact, they are.

The second obligation of leadership is to ensure that a continuous stream of information is being delivered from leaders to members. This information is not just the traditional kind about programs, activities, and benefits. More important, it involves effectively communicating the rationale behind policy-making and direction setting. Successful association leaders understand it is their obligation not just to communicate what judgments have been rendered, but also to create opportunities for every member to see, feel, understand, and appreciate the basis of judgments that have been made on their behalf.

When leaders fulfill this two-way obligation, they are constructing a relationship of parity with members. The relationship is characterized by partnership and peerism. They are creating a better balance between leadership's view of the world and the view of the world held by the membership. When information systems are established and maintained to institutionalize this exchange of critical information among an association's key stakeholders, we refer to the association's operational philosophy as "knowledge-based." The most successful associations of the 21st century will be "knowledge-based" in their governance and operational functioning. We believe this organizational environment will be both preferred for successful execution of the 21st-century competencies, and the organizational climate that most demands and cherishes them.

Groups of People as Volunteers

Associations are groups of people who *voluntarily* come together; they are essentially volunteer-intensive operations even when membership is automatic or required by law. It is this aspect of associations that most makes the association dynamic (whether the association is for-profit or not-for-profit) different from the dynamic of public or for-profit institutions.

In an association, unlike a corporation or government agency, the volunteer portion of the work force doesn't have to do anything it doesn't want to do. The traditional concepts of motivation, as they are employed in the typical workplace, do not apply . Traditional motivation theory uses extrinsic reward; that is, "If you do your job you will be rewarded; if you don't do your job you will be penalized." This theory does not work in an association.

Consider this example: The committee chair who does an extraordinary job. The chair calls the committee together when it is supposed to be called together; leads the committee through deliberation with effective group process; guides the committee rather than directing it to a preconceived notion; and has the committee explore context and options, investigate advantages and disadvantages, and select the best alternative. The group produces a report that is sound, viable, understandable, and lucid for presentation to the board of directors. And, the chair has already organized the committee members to continue to support the proposal once it is initiated. What a wonderful committee chair! What is the typical reward for such exceptional performance? A letter of appreciation? If it is a good budget year, a plaque? Another assignment that gives that person more work?

Let's look at a reverse situation. The committee chair is not effective. This person seldom calls the committee together. When convened, there is really no effective discussion at the meeting. The group is used as a vehicle for pursuing a personal agenda. The committee's time is spent in confrontation, not collaboration; in conflict, not cooperation. The report is hardly understandable and inappropriate. While the committee chair pressures the board to adopt the recommendation, several members of the committee are lobbying against it on the telephone.

How do we recognize that performance? Give them a letter of appreciation? A plaque? Another assignment? So much for distinguishing effective and ineffective behavior with traditional extrinsic rewards and motivation.

Successful leaders of associations take a different approach toward inspiring performance among volunteers. This approach can be called "wantivation." Wantivation involves intrinsic reward. It promotes initiative from the inside, rather than from the outside. Wantivation occurs when the volunteer comes to believe that it is in his or her own self-interest to be actively involved, to accept responsibility, and to fulfill that responsibility effectively. The behaviors employed in order to wantivate volunteers include creating a clear and inspiring vision of the way we want the world to be because of their actions, and allowing volunteers to decide on the contributions they can and are willing to make in order for this vision to become a reality. This behavioral reality in associations is increasing in significance as generational and other demographic changes in membership alter the values, attitudes, and preferences of large segments of current and prospective members. The evolving demands of the executive's employers and employees, related to the values and work climate of the organization with which they are involved, underline the essential nature of the relational 21st-century competencies identified in this study.

Common Self-Interest

Another key concept reflected in our definition of an association is the notion of commonness—common problems, common needs, and common goals. *An effective association is one that recognizes and focuses on the common self-interests of its members.* The (a) identification, (b) affirmation, (c) allocation of resources to, (d) pursuit, (e) achievement, and (f) celebration of the common self-interest are essential characteristics of effective associations.

It is a sense of self-interest that calls members to become involved in an association; something of sufficient importance for someone to voluntarily become a member. By their very nature, individual self-interests vary greatly from person to person. In an association, the common self-interests are those certain basic interests shared by all. The common self-interest represents the fundamental purpose for which members have voluntarily decided to associate with each other.

Successful association leaders understand the importance of recognizing and focusing on the common self-interest of members. If this is not done, two unhappy scenarios can usually result.

The Conflict Syndrome

The conflict syndrome occurs when leadership fails to attend to the common self-interest. The basic symptoms of the syndrome are quite visible: board meetings where more time is spent arguing over who should make a decision than is actually spent on making the decision itself; committee meetings where every member of the committee believes that every other member of the committee has a hidden agenda; or budget deliberations where much energy is consumed in deciding how to distribute a shrinking amount of capital among a growing number of special interest groups.

Ultimately, the conflict syndrome leads to organizational paralysis. The association loses the ability to focus attention and energy on things that are significant. Only the simple, unimportant things avoid objection by some group. The association loses its ability to muster sufficient energy to address the real problems and opportunities faced by its members. Eventually, the organization is known as a group that has little to offer and little influence to wield. At that point, the benefit that accrues to members significantly diminishes. Active involvement decreases noticeably. It is only a matter of time before membership numbers diminish as well.

The Peanut Butter Syndrome

Whether staff or volunteer, the acceptance of the responsibility of leadership in an association involves judgments about the allocation of resources. A useful metaphor is agreeing to be a member of a group assigned to spread peanut butter on a loaf of bread. For most associations, there is a predetermined limitation involved in completing the assignment—a limited amount of peanut butter to be spread across a piece of bread that appears to still be rising.

Associations want to serve the needs of their members. When a member comes to the association and says, "I have a problem," it is natural for the leadership to say, "Let's hear the problem and see if we can help." Or when a group of members come with a long list of good ideas, leadership is likely to say, "Let's hear the ideas; we'll try to do something with them; we are dedicated to being inclusive here." Soon, the peanut butter is being spread thinner and thinner.

Eventually, it is spread so thinly across the bread that no matter where you bite down, you cannot taste the peanut butter.

This condition is created by a failure to focus on common self-interest. Limited resources are so broadly distributed across so many initiatives that the most significant needs and desires of any significant segment of members are not accomplished with any degree of excellence. Again, the association faces diminished member benefit, decreased active involvement, and declining membership.

It is leadership's ability to identify, focus, and act on the common self-interests of membership—not trying to be all things to all people—that most often results in sustained association effectiveness. For most associations, achieving and maintaining consensus on what will constitute success is paradoxically becoming both increasingly essential and increasingly difficult.

As membership grows, it also tends to become more diverse. Demographic changes, especially intergenerational and multicultural membership populations, will continue to expand both the number and variation of "self-interests," attitudes, and preferences present in an association. Simultaneously, an increasingly complex and interrelated world will present an ever-growing number of possible items for an association's attention. The confluence of these two phenomena will create a leadership dilemma requiring a level of mastery of the 21st-century competencies related to information and consensus building that surpasses the already difficult demands of today.

Exhibit 1: Life Stages of an Association

Eight Stages in the Life of an Association

Conception: A group of people see an advantage to voluntarily coming together and start an association.

Infancy: The founders are still in charge as the organization struggles to survive. Every job requires more work than the founders can do.

Puberty: The organization grows steadily but suffers from awkwardness in its dealings with outsiders and with internal coordination. Entrepreneurial skills are gradually replaced by more professional management techniques and skills.

Young Adulthood: Accepted management practices are implemented, including formalized personnel practices. The beginnings of bureaucracy and internal politics are evident.

Adulthood: The organization is mastering its environment and serving the needs of its members. Management is peaking and preparing to expand, enter new areas of service, or add new functions.

Late Adulthood: The excitement of the organization has diminished. The membership will not support innovation. A complacent atmosphere lacking any sense of urgency or zeal prevails.

Old Age: The organization is losing its ability to cope with its environment and serve the real needs of its members. Managers and leaders bicker, and internal control is lacking. All of a sudden, things seem to come apart, and few people seem to care.

REVITALIZATION/OBSCURITY/DISSOLUTION
Adapted, with permission of the publisher from
Leadership: Strategies for Organizational Effectiveness
by James J. Cribben, ©1981 AMACOM, a Division of the
American Management Association. All rights reserved.

The Organizational Lifecycle

Associations tend to migrate through eight basic stages throughout their cycles of evolution (see Exhibit 1). Understanding these stages is a tool used by successful leadership to create direction, guide the organization, and achieve desired results. It is important to understand that there is no universal law that requires every association to move through these stages in a particular order or to spend a certain amount of time in any stage. In fact, these passages are more cyclical than linear, and it is certainly, though unfortunately, possible for an association to move directly from infancy to old age in a few short years. It is also probable that a complex association will exhibit some of the characteristics of one stage and some of the characteristics of another stage since in a complex association, various programs and services will be in varying life stages themselves.

What is important is understanding that each stage carries with it a set of behavioral characteristics that call upon particular leadership qualities and actions in differing degrees.

It is logical that the distinction between stages is mostly behavioral. Associations are essentially people-intensive organizations. As an enterprise, it serves people and it gets its work done through people. Associations are not capital intensive or machine intensive. An association's mission is accomplished when people do things, and, for that reason, its most important capital is its human capital. It should be no surprise that, in a people-intensive organization, it is primarily the behavior of people that defines the life condition or life stage of the organization. Appreciating these dynamics can be critical to the success of an association. It is also good news for leadership because it suggests that a decision can be made to revitalize at any point by making an educated commitment to alter the behavior exhibited by people leading and working within the organization. As the relevant world of any association changes with increasing speed and unpredictability, the capability of leadership to rapidly adjust the organization to dramatic changes in its environment will become increasingly critical to sustaining success. The

21st century will require enhanced sophistication in executive competency related to coherently managing an organization that must be more fluid and flexible than ever before to maintain responsiveness in a frequently shifting environment.

Let's examine each life stage more closely.

Conception and Infancy: The start-up of any organization or new project takes passion and hands-on blood, sweat, and tears. It requires a focused desire to make something happen, energy, and the capital necessary to make it so. Associations, however, are notorious for undercapitalizing new ventures by trying to simultaneously launch a variety of new programs—all on a shoestring. This is bad news for members who will benefit most from an association's program or service when it reaches the more mature of stages of young adulthood and adulthood. Why? Because when an organization or a program is in the developmental stages, it is not yet providing significant tangible benefits to many of the members supporting it. If it takes too long to push the program or organization to young adulthood, the initiative loses momentum, incentive, and support, decreasing the probability that the new initiative will be successful. It will take too long to get to the point where someone says, "This is a great value." In the worst case scenario, by the time the program is positioned to effectively respond to a need or opportunity, the problem has changed or the opportunity has evaporated.

This stage of development requires entrepreneurial spirit, risk-taking, and action-oriented people. It requires aggressive fundraisers and membership recruiters, people who are willing to look at impossible tasks and find uncommon solutions.

Puberty: Awkwardness and identity confusion typify associations in the puberty stage, because it is a time of development when the organization is often disproportionately concerned about its appearance. The organization is building an identity and image for itself for the first time. In the beginning, the self-image is often based on what the group wants other people or important groups to think about it.

Adolescents tend to be involved in testing and experimenting with their world to learn good judgment and discernment. They may do things for the sake of immediate self-satisfaction or to be more liked by someone whose opinion they think is important, even though the behavior may have significant negative consequences to them in the future. They sometimes lack the experience to understand that something you do today can be a problem tomorrow—that no one is invulnerable.

An association in the puberty stage of development often faces similar issues. Three concepts important to leaders of organizations in this stage are: identity, image, and name.

- **Identity** is who you are. It is the sum total of the association's mission, core membership, program of work, and accomplishments.
- **Image** is how people think of you, and that may or may not be commensurate with the identity an association desires.
- **Name** is what an association calls itself. The objective is to have a name that contributes to an image commensurate with the desired identity.

Leadership is usually called upon in this stage to provide systematic order, boundaries, and rules to sustain the organization. It is critical that the organization stay focused on the common self-interests of the members, avoiding the temptation to be what it thinks will impress or please others. In the 21st century, as units of the organization become more diverse, it will also be important for leaders to be able to sustain direction by focusing on desired outcomes with at least as much and probably more emphasis than previously placed on boundaries, requirements, and procedures.

Young Adulthood: This is usually a time of excitement, innovation, and high member enthusiasm and participation. Systems are in place to sustain the organization and accepted management practices are implemented, including effective personnel practices. There is now something of which many people are very proud.

This also tends to be the time when power struggles begin to emerge. It is usually the beginning of bureaucracy and internal politics. The challenge to leadership is to keep the group focused on the mission and goals of the organization, rather than consuming valuable energy in power struggles.

During both the puberty and young adulthood stages, what we call "systems leadership" is of importance. Systems leaders are team-oriented people who appreciate the mechanics of the organization. They give attention to process and how things get done.

Adulthood: In adulthood, the association is mastering its environment and serving the needs of its members. Management is strong and the organization is often preparing to expand by entering new areas of service or adding new functions.

It is in adulthood that members achieve the greatest value for their investment in the association. The challenge for leadership is to maintain adulthood, and it is strategic leadership that is designed for the task. Strategic leaders tend to be far-sighted, conceptual thinkers. They are people open to change and willing to continually reinvent the organization and its services to respond to the ever-changing needs of its members. Leadership failure in this stage makes the association vulnerable to organization wide late adulthood and old age.

Late Adulthood and Old Age: The excitement of the association is diminishing. The members will not support innovation, and there is an atmosphere of complacency lacking any sense of urgency or zeal.

If this continues it ultimately leads to old age: The organization has lost its ability to cope with its environment and serve the real needs of its members. Leaders, members, and staff bicker; internal control is lacking. Soon everything comes apart, and very few people seem to care.

In stages of late adulthood and old age it is critical that transformational leadership be applied. This is leadership that is willing to take a risk, willing to rock the boat. Transformational leadership creates an environment within which new ideas and perspectives are brought to reshaping and revitalizing deadened services, structures, or behaviors.

In the 21st century, strategic management of the organization's resources—its "peanut butter"—will be critical to achieving coherency in an environment of rapid and complex change. The successful association executive of tomorrow will need to knowledgeably monitor the overall condition of the organization's business lines and operations, in light of the evolving dynamics. Twenty first-century competencies related to understanding complex relationships, using information, and deploying resources will be prerequisites for continually navigating the association's program portfolio through stages to maximize the benefits accorded to members and other stakeholders.

The Life Stages Applied to Programs

Most association leaders, when asked to wave a magic wand and select the life stage they would most like for their association, select adulthood with a healthy dose of young adulthood. It depicts an organization providing quality service and value to its members, while continually being revitalized by innovation and enthusiasm. Energy and responsiveness are dynamically being applied to a changing environment.

Experience and research suggests that the most successful associations tend to exhibit a certain proportion of their program of work in one or another of these stages. Imagine the various programs and organization components of an association; for example, the annual convention, the major publication, an education program, or the chapter system. It is probable that each of these areas is in a distinctly identifiable life stage itself.

We have observed over time that the most successful organizations tend to maintain a particular proportion of their overall portfolio in one or another life stage at any given time. In most successful associations, between 15% and 20% of the program portfolio appears to be between conception and young adulthood, but not yet entering young adulthood. These are new programs being undertaken to respond to changes in the environment and member needs. (Note: Only a few years ago, the proportion of the portfolio in these early stages was 10% to 15%. We believe this increase reflects the increased velocity of change being experienced by associations and their members.) These programs should be pushed into young adulthood and adulthood as quickly as possible.

Between 60% and 80% of the program portfolio is generally in the stages of young adulthood and adulthood. This proportion is critically important to the health and vitality of the organization because, as we have stated earlier, this is when members receive the greatest tangible benefits and value.

Even in the program portfolios of successful associations, there are some programs heading through late adulthood and old age. In most associations this seems to be somewhere between 10% and 15%. What distinguishes successful associations from others is their ability to turn these programs into "old friends," rather than sources of confrontation, conflict, and consternation by positioning them as successes upon which the next generation of programs is being built

There are three conditions that will cause a program or service to move through late adulthood into old age.

- A program created in the past to meet a need that no longer exists.
- A program created in the past to meet a need that still exists, but the way in which the association is meeting that need is no longer the best way. There is now a better way to meet the need and, usually, someone else is doing it.
- A program created in the past to meet a need that still exists; the association is still meeting the need in the best way possible; but the number or proportion of the membership who perceive it as a high priority has significantly decreased

over time. There is no longer sufficient economy of scale to provide the program at the same level of excellence that its loyal users have come to expect.

In all three cases, the program is headed for late adulthood and old age. It is unlikely that any delivery or promotion innovation can rescue the product from its almost inevitable demise.

The real question is how to overcome exit barriers and convert these programs to "old friends." An exit barrier is something that makes it difficult for you to leave out of a program once you've gotten into it. For example, an exit barrier exists if the association has become dependent upon the program as a source of revenue to fund other things. Therefore, exiting will mean either finding another source of revenue or reducing expenditures on other things.

Another exit barrier is often our affections, though not necessarily our affections for the program. Frequently, a significant program is associated with a very appreciated and well-respected veteran member or members who view the program as their personal contribution to the industry or profession. They may even perceive any critical discussion of it to be a direct assault upon them as individuals. The strategy of choice here might be to focus on the change as something that naturally results because of the contributions of that "old friend."

For leaders, it is almost always more successful when managing evolution and innovation if the change is positioned as a logical extension of what has been working for the organization, as opposed to positioning that change as a declaration that there's a terrible problem that needs to be fixed or that people have been doing something wrong. Assaults on tradition and values, especially in generationally diverse associations, tend to invite defensiveness and coalesce opposition to innovation. Successful leaders celebrate what the association is emerging from and, in so doing, turn traditional supporters of the targeted program into partners in change, rather than obstructers.

Association leaders who are able to do this are then able to reallocate or reinvest this 10% to 15% of the organization's energy and resources into new programs or fund innovations and modifications in programs in the adulthood stages to keep them vital.

A relevant allegory can help us understand how critical this dynamic can be to the health, vitality, and sometimes survival of an association.

Many years ago, there was an association called the Society for Hammer and Chisels. It was dedicated to teaching people to use hammers and chisels and to advising the makers of hammers and chisels on how to construct them in a way that was most beneficial to users. Anyone who used a hammer and chisel could belong, so there were woodcarvers, stonecarvers, mechanics, and neurosurgeons.

This association did very well for many years and grew rapidly by providing major benefits to its members. The entrepreneurs who started the organization tended to remain in charge because they were the leaders for a long time and provided a historic view.

One day something important occurred—the invention of the drill. Some of the members began to realize that the drill could make a hole more quickly and with more precision than they had ever been able to with a hammer and chisel. These members went to the leadership and said, "What about the drill?" The leaders responded with a shrug, "What about it? It's a fad, a passing fancy. The hammer and chisel has always worked for us, and it will continue to work for us. There may be some advantages to the drill, but we are hammer and chisel people. That's what we are, what we do, that's our identity."

The members went along with this for a while until the subsequent invention of the electric drill. Some of the younger members of the association said, "Wait a minute, what about the electric drill? We're using it, and we know that it makes holes faster, more precisely, and with much less energy than the hammer and chisel or the manual drill." The leadership said, "Yeah, we understand that, but take our word for it, it's a fad just like TV. It will never catch on. We are about hammers and chisels; that's what we'll always do; we're comfortable with it."

This time the younger members of the organization waved good-bye and formed their own association called the Society for the Advancement of Drilling. The new society became competitors of the original organization, causing the Society for the Hammer and Chisel to lose many members.

The new organization had learned some valuable lessons. They engaged in sound planning and policy processes. They had task forces looking at the future and the needs of the membership. These task forces gathered information, made projections, and began to educate the members—creating awareness and understanding and providing information about the future—and then moving in to train the members, while continually "looking around the corner" to anticipate what might be coming next. (In other words, they had learned to maintain a continuous stream of information to and from their members that kept pace with the changes in the members' world.)

Not surprisingly, the new society did very well and was fully prepared when on the horizon appeared the laser wand. The strategic planning group discovered it and was fascinated by its potential; just by pushing a button, you could make a more precise hole better and quicker than you ever could with any drill or hammer and chisel. In fact, it was so great that you could even make a hole behind something that you did not want to make a hole in. This, the group speculated, was a wonderful innovation that would transform how its members worked and who its members would be.

The society's leaders began to alter its program to keep pace with the emerging new reality so dramatically affecting their industry, its professions, and the identity of the association. They also did one other thing. They changed their name to the Society for the Advancement of Holes.

What is the moral of the story? Focus on the outcome. Understand that an effective 21st-century association may need to be prepared to change the basic dynamics of the organization in response to significant environmental changes, not just tinker with a specific product, result or problem. The implications of this emerging new reality to the role, function, and tools of tomorrow's association executive are reflected in the set of competencies suggested as especially critical for the 21st century.

Associations as Systems

Individual associations do not exist in a vacuum. They exist in a context that includes a variety of events, phenomena, and occurrences that constantly affect the needs of members. When a significant change occurs in that context, the needs of the members will change. For example, a change in the members' workplace or marketplace, a change in demographics, a change in technology or science that provides a new or different tool or challenge, a change in the economic environment, or a change in the social values exhibited in the communities in which members are operating— any of these changes in the realities of the larger world will change the needs of an association's members, thereby changing the association itself.

Associations exist to meet the needs of the membership. The first step in understanding associations as systems is to identify what those needs are and to recognize that each change in the external reality means needs will have changed and must be reassessed. It is only after, and based on, this assessment that leaders are able to effectively set the direction of the association.

Direction is articulated in the mission, goals, and strategy of the association. Mission is a clear, concise, and inspiring expression of the fundamental reason for the organization's existence. It is not just a statement of what the organization does or how it does it. Mission states who the organization is and why it exists.

Exhibit 2: Associations as Systems

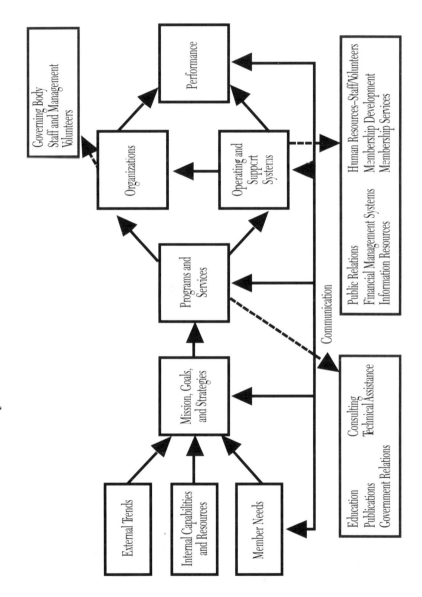

Goals are statements that describe the condition or attribute the organization seeks to attain. Goals are not statements of what the organization is going to do, i.e., what business lines it is in or what programs are offered. Goals are statements that describe in tangible ways how the relevant world will be different as a result of whatever the organization does. They create a clear and understandable picture of what success will look like. In goals, vision integrates with strategy in the statement of organization direction. Goals are derived from the vision leaders and members have articulated to describe the future they desire.

With direction based on the needs of members within the context of external reality, the organization is prepared to identify strategies for goal achievement. Strategies are the bridge between direction and action. They represent how the association will organize and focus its resources and actions to maximize effectiveness and efficiency in achieving goals. It is at this point that the organization is ready to consider the programs and services it will offer, the business lines it will be in, and how it will allocate its time and resources.

With the program portfolio devised, the association is prepared to think about how it should organize itself. What governance structure, committee structure, financial structure, or staff structure and what operating and support systems will create efficiency in executing strategies selected to achieve the desired outcomes?

Central to understanding associations as systems is the concept of *effective* and *efficient*. *Efficient* is the answer to the question, "Are we doing things right?" *Effective* is the answer to the question, "Are we doing the right things?"

We believe a critical success factor in the 21st century will be leadership's ability to coherently identify the right things to do, and partner with the experience, expertise, and time of staff and committees to identify how to do things right. Unfortunately, it is very easy to be highly efficient while doing all the wrong things, moving with all deliberate speed to all the wrong places, and arriving there much faster than anyone thought possible. The unfolding realities of the 21st century reinforce the importance of doing the right things, even if occasionally doing them the wrong way, rather than doing the wrong things right.

When leadership has clearly identified the needs of the members in their current and emerging environment, clearly articulated what success will look like, and organized to achieve that success, then the association is best positioned to produce positive results. When an association produces positive results, two things will happen. The world in which the members operate will change as a result of the association's efforts, and/or the members will be empowered to be more successful in their world. In either case, member needs are altered, at least in part, as a result of the work of the association.

When the needs of the members change, whether because of positive results of the association's efforts, or because of unanticipated external changes, everything else will be affected as well. Consequently, the association must again reassess its direction, its strategies, its program of work, and how it is organized. In other words, success in an association contributes to maintaining a dynamic of constant change in the organization as a system.

In effective associations of the 21st century, leaders will understand that the need for change is as often caused by success as it is caused by a problem. It will not simply be the task of leadership to fix something that has gone wrong. Often it will be positioning to provide new services in response to something that has gone right. The only associations where leadership will not have to continually manage through the dynamic of constant change will be those associations that do very little for their members. Since little is being done for the members, the members' needs will rarely change. Such associations will continue to do what they have always done before, rather than examine what they need to do to ensure that tomorrow will be as successful as the today created by yesterday's decisions. Avoiding this means (a) continually reassessing the external environment and member needs; (b) realigning mission, goals, and strategy; and (c) organizing in new ways that promote goal achievement. Simply put, it means there are no sacred cows in the successful association of the 21st century.

Leadership Roles and Responsibilities

In effective organizations, whether for-profit or not-for-profit, the chief executive officer engages in certain identifiable activities designed to contribute certain things to the organization's dynamic. These activities include looking at today in terms of the picture being created of a preferable tomorrow and focusing on that vision; looking at the implications of today in moving toward that vision; thinking about how to align and integrate discreet but related parts of the organization into a common whole; getting problems out of the way of the work force, whether paid or volunteer; inspiring, motivating, and building commitment; representing the organization in the marketplace, with peer groups, and with other organizations; and being accountable to the customers and owners of the organization for performance. These activities are also the essential roles of an organization's chief executive officer.

One of the fundamental ways an association differs from a for-profit enterprise is that in an association, the actual execution of the chief executive officer's role is most often shared between a chief staff executive and a chief elected officer. The implications of this arrangement are enormous. If the relationship between these two partners is not positive, constructive, aware, and dynamic, the association will be left without effective execution of the chief executive roles. If the relationship is a sound one, operating in harmonious and respectful partnership to execute the roles of chief executive, then the organization will enjoy a key element required for success.

Our study and this book focus on the critical competencies of 21st-century association executives. One of the competencies examined in detail is the ability of the executive to establish and maintain healthy relationships. This, of course, includes critical relationships with elected leaders. It is equally essential to organizational success, however, that the volunteer leadership of associations exhibit identical commitment and capacity. Volunteer leaders need to create an environment that supports the executive's ability to demonstrate and apply these competencies in the work of the association. *This means a willingness to move beyond traditional definitions of territorial roles and authority. It means redefining the working relationship between staff and volunteers.*

The Balance of Power

One of the considerations dominating the conversations of association leaders over the years has been about the balance of power. Is the association member driven, volunteer driven, or staff driven? As we move toward the 21st century, it is becoming apparent that the most successful associations are moving beyond this traditional focus of a clear hierarchical distribution of power to consider how to be a knowledge-based association.

Let's consider the continuum of power portraits found in Exhibit 3. In considering the profile definitions, the differentiating factors are in whose interests and on what basis decisions are made. For example, in the snapshot descriptions of the *staff-driven* or *officer-driven* associations, decisions are made based on what is best for the decision makers. In *staff-directed* or *need-driven* organizations, decisions are made based on what is best for the association and its corporate survival. In a *product-driven* association, decisions are made based on what will sell and what will generate the greatest revenues. *Member-responsive* associations make decisions based on member wants and needs.

Exhibit 3: Balance of Power—A Continuum

Staff Driven	Staff Directed	Product Driven	Market Directed	Member Responsive	Need Driven	Officer Driven

	Trends Toward Staff Driven	Trends Toward Volunteer Driven
PROS	❏ Efficiency ❏ Consistency of direction ❏ Professional expertise	❏ Involvement and participation ❏ Volunteer expertise ❏ Lower staff costs ❏ Understand member needs
CONS	❏ Low involvement ❏ Lack of commitment ❏ Less member appreciation of effort ❏ Staff on defensive	❏ Decision time ❏ Roles/responsibilities ❏ Getting work done ❏ Less stable leadership ❏ Higher meeting costs

(No Right Answer)

All of these decision profiles share the use of beliefs and perceptions as a basis for decisions. A relevant and rational data base of information on which to base decisions is absent or unused, and the quality of decisions is extremely dependent on the quality of the beliefs and perceptions of decision makers. The absence of a quality, credible, and reliable data base often leads to discomfort and power struggles among potential decision-making groups. The association making decisions without the benefit of a common, defensible information base is particularly vulnerable to the pluralization or polarization of interests that can easily occur when different power groups are operating from dissimilar views of the relevant world.

Our research suggests that the most successful associations of the future will be, and will continue to move toward, the market-directed and ultimately the knowledge-based profile. In this organizational portrait, who makes the decision is not nearly as important as the quality of information on which decisions are made (see Exhibit 4). A rational, common data base is developed and maintained to guide decisions about member wants, needs, and preferences. Members and staff at all levels are engaged in continuous and integrated consideration of (a) member needs, (b) strategic position of the organization, and (c) external marketplace dynamics and realities. The organization demonstrates a commitment to the collection and sharing of information—not just raw data. It provides decision makers of all types with the quality of perception, the credibility, and the relevant information needed to make sound and understandable decisions. It allows decision making to occur at the point in the organization where the decision can best be made, as defined by need rather than by hierarchy or territory. These associations   will be able to reinvest energy formerly spent on worrying about who has the right to make a decision. This valuable energy will be rechanneled into additional services and activity to better meet member needs.

Associations of different shapes and sizes, because of the basic nature of the enterprise, share many characteristics and dynamics in common. Understanding the special nature of associations as complex organizations will be an increasingly critical competency for all association leaders. It is also a particular and peculiar context within which executive competencies of the 21st century must be developed and employed.

Exhibit 4: Balance of Power—Profiles

Staff Driven

Staff makes decisions based on what the staff believes is best for the staff.

Staff Directed

Staff makes decisions based on what the staff believes is best for the association.

Product Driven

Staff makes decisions based on their perceptions of member needs, and what existing or revised products would meet those needs at desired revenue levels.

Knowledge Based

Who makes the decision is not nearly as important as the quality of the information on which decisions are made. A rational, common data base is developed and maintained to guide decisions about member wants, needs, and preferences. Members and staff at all levels are engaged in continuous and integrated consideration of (a) member needs, (b) strategic position of the organization, and (c) external marketplace dynamics and realities.

Market Driven

Member and staff leadership make decisions about what they think is best for the membership based upon limited information about member wants. High-level strategy is often not reflected in program decisions or activity at the work level.

Member Responsive

The leadership oligarchy makes decisions based on its perceptions of what members want and need.

Need Driven

The leadership oligarchy makes decisions based on what it believes is best for the association.

Officer Driven

The leadership oligarchy makes decisions based on what it believes is best for the leadership.

Key

Wants —The benefits or outcomes desired.

Needs Activity required to provide benefits and/or achieve outcomes.

Preferences—Most attractive attributes of products, services, communications, and delivery systems.

CHAPTER 3
Why Good Executives Get Fired

I n recent years two significant and disturbing trends have been observed. A number of association executives commonly accepted as successful and often commonly accepted by their colleagues as models for the profession have been fired. At the same time, a number of associations, particularly large trade associations, are frequently turning to their own industry experts for leadership rather than hiring from the association management profession.

To understand the dynamics at work when good executives get fired, it is critical to view those dynamics in context. One contextual principal is "what is perceived to be, is." That means that the individuals with whom executives interact—whether subordinates, colleagues, or superordinates—will make judgments, decisions, and form opinions primarily on what they perceive to be the case. The important point here is that behavior, particularly in an association, no matter how crazy, has a logical basis.

The association executive's measure of success depends almost entirely upon how other people perceive him or her. Sometimes those perceptions will not be based in fact. That doesn't matter. These judgments are based entirely upon the information available, and the two primary sources of available information within an association are a) personal experiences and b) information gathered from other individuals whose judgment is trusted or with whom behavioral or political coalitions have been formed.

A second contextual principal is that in the absence of information based on the truth, activists and agitators, whether well-meaning or not, develop assumptions to explain what they believe they are seeing. Those perceptions may be founded on inaccurate, out-of-date, irrelevant information, or on assumptions constructed in the absence of information. But it doesn't matter, because "what is perceived, is."

The Symptoms

Associations in which these situations are likely to lead to trouble for the association executive exhibit several observable symptoms. The symptoms apply in all types of organizations, regardless of the gender of the executive, the size of the group, its location, or the nature of its business lines.

There is a lack of explicit consensus within the leadership about what constitutes success.

The absence of a clear and common definition of what success will look like creates the opportunity for good executives to be fired. For example, leadership might define success as better serving the existing membership, while the executive may feel aggressively growing the membership is the primary measure of success. Absent agreement on what constitutes achievement, other things like management style, personality traits, or the personal biases of influential members will be used to judge whether the executive is performing effectively.

There are internal and external conditions present that promote dissatisfaction with performance or result in dismissal.

External conditions often include a membership functioning in a business environment where a) there is chaos, as has been the case in the financial industry; b) chaos is expected in the foreseeable future, such as the impact of health care delivery changes on the medical community; or c) an unpredictable future is creating extraordinary anxiety for a significant portion of the membership, as in information professions, where personal expertise may be replaced by smart computer software. The members are extremely anxious because they have no sense of their own future. That lack of agreement about what the future holds invites internal squabbling at all organizational levels about how best to prepare for the unknown. There is often continuous confrontation and conflict within the organization, resulting in political and personal posturing. The organization's energy tends to be internally directed toward judgments about politics and personality and less externally directed to executing programs and policies in the best interests of members. This exacerbates anxiety as members feel that both their own world and their organization are spinning out of control.

There is a lack of trust.
When we asked chief staff executives who were fired what happened, they usually said, "There was a lack of trust." Chief elected officers said the same thing. Loss of trust is the code, the comfortable label. It is often the side effect of either or both of the first two symptoms.

Common Causes
Several causes emerge as commonly contributing to create the above symptoms. The first is *an executive who functions knowledgeably but behaves ineffectively.* For the purposes of this study a "good executive" is defined as a) having a content knowledge of all the appropriate job responsibilities of an executive, b) having a track record of professional activity within the association community, and c) having sufficient professional association experience at a significant enough level to be chief staff officer or senior staff. These characteristics tend to earn the executive recognition within the association management community. Historically, they are the combination of behaviors that have been acknowledged and rewarded. It is when this knowledge is applied ineffectively that trouble begins. Intellectual judgment about a given situation may be

sound, but how it is executed is inappropriate for the situation. For example, the executive who knows when it is appropriate to disagree with his or her board chair on a significant issue, but doesn't know when it is inappropriate to have the disagreement in public or how to broach the issue with behaviors that promote an accepting attitude rather than a defensive display of angry authority. A short series of such behavioral dissonance in a visible situation is often the first moment of truth that leads to a decision to dismiss. Often, these practitioners have understood but been unable to execute the behaviors that bring success in the critical competency areas of managing knowledge and relationships.

A second common cause is *an executive who appears to confuse manipulation with leadership.* What is the difference? If people would not be supportive if they knew all of the information available to the executive or if the real intention were acknowledged, then that is manipulation. If information is used to create awareness, inform debate, build consensus on outcome and strategies, and motivate actions, then that is leadership.

The third common cause is *the executive who appears to be more concerned with his or her role as an executive and the nature of the job than with doing a good job for members.* These are often individuals whose self-esteem depends heavily on how their peers and others view them. If these individuals view their own community primarily as other association professionals, instead of the group of individuals who employ them, they make judgments based upon the expected reactions of their professional colleagues as opposed to the anticipated reactions of their members. That might mean an executive spends significant time in lobbying association causes because his or her peers value it, even though influencing public policy is purposefully not a part of their own association's mission. It doesn't matter if there is no real conflict of interest. The problem is the executive is visibly engaged in spending time on something the members don't value or may even reject as not worthy.

The fourth common cause is *the executive who tries to grow the association beyond what its members want or need it to be.* Often focus is shifted from serving member needs to issues of organizational size, initiative, or sophistication preferred by the executive. The most cost-effective benefit for members is perceived to have been sacrificed for professional reputation and status.

Each of these causes is often perceived by member leaders as an absence of service values and leads directly to loss of trust. When the relationship reaches this point, turnaround is virtually impossible.

From the Perspective of the Fired Executive

There were also common descriptions among executives of what in fact was the real contributing problem. These most often included:

- "Something is really very wrong with the governance process."
- "New models are needed in order for the association executive to function effectively."
- "I was the victim of a decision-making process that didn't fit today's reality."
- "It's hard to get competent and talented volunteers."
- "Elected leaders must be taught to value the profession of association management."

Whether accurate observations or not, the executive of the 21st century who seeks to be successful is well advised to look within for solutions to these problems, rather than be victim to circumstances.

Contributing Conditions

Preceding the common causes of lack of consensus, confusion, and resulting loss of trust, there are often indirect contributing conditions paving the way for dissatisfaction and dismissal. *These contributing conditions all share in common a failure to maintain clear consensus on what constitutes success.* In the absence of such clarity, using irrelevant benchmarks to judge success becomes the only alternative. If the association hasn't been clear about what outcomes it wants, what is often used for appraisal is comfort with the style the executive exhibits, the role he or she appears to have chosen, or perceptions of personal loyalty to the membership powers of the moment.

Associations choose how they will spend their limited energies. *If the organization's energy tends to be directed toward internal power and political issues of importance to the leadership oligarchy, rather than issues of direct service to the members, the probability of a good executive eventually being fired increases dramatically.*

This probability is also increased *if there is a lack of transactional partnership among the people or groups with power.* Such organizations are characterized by hierarchy and turf protection rather than collaboration. People are more concerned with maintaining boundaries and preserving power and prerogative, than with collaboration to accomplish clearly defined common and desirable ends. Such organizations are also characterized by relationships that are dependent rather than interdependent. The organization almost always tends to be personality driven, rather than driven by market research and stated outcomes. It is seldom supported by systematic approaches for decision making and resource allocation. They are often historic bastions of the "great man/woman" theory. Because they are personality driven, two things happen. First, leadership focuses its sights on things that can be done during the period of time when the personality is in place, rather than focusing on those things of real importance to members that require more time to complete. This lowers their gaze as a service provider or leader. At the same time, the emphasis on political visibility is raised. Decisions about the program of work are made not on the basis of significance of the contribution, but on the basis of how little risk is involved with the smallest amount of effort to accomplish the biggest thing that can be seen by the greatest number of people.

Absence or atrophy of systemic communications channels is also a contributing condition to increasing the probability of dismissal. In associations, information is currency. It is both how we lead and the essence of our primary business lines. In the organizations we studied, three things happened. First, communications channels were non-functional or poorly functioning, usually as a result of underinvestment. (Where there is no transactional partnership, there is no need to make sure everyone stays informed. All the executive needs to do is make sure the powerful individuals whose behavior he or she wishes to influence know.)

Second, was a pro forma use of communication channels. Discussions of superficial issues or outright avoidance was the rule. The right kinds of things were discussed in meetings, just not in the right kind of way. As an example, if the board's agenda contains an item on public policy, the focus of discussion is on who will present the testimony, not on the content of the statement. Or in a discussion of the year's education program, only the promotion, location, and schedule are discussed, rather than identification of what member needs are being met or how the program portfolio contributes to the overall organizational vision and strategy. As a result of pro forma use of communications, the real decision was tightly controlled by small groups of power, and board actions were left only to rubber stamp or micro-edit the actions of others.

And finally, we observed an avoidance of legitimate opposition. Side negotiations and discussions were the norm. The substantive and significant information was not put through systemic communication channels.

Significant Dilemmas Create a Fishbowl

Both governance and leadership involve making choices in areas where there are seldom clear cut, either/or choices. Rather, balanced positions must be chosen on a continuum of choices. The inability of an executive to recognize the implications of those choices and guide governance through them often created a fishbowl with the executive's intellectual, communications, and behavioral competencies on display.

We are not aware of an association where a good executive was fired when the organization was moving toward being market-directed or knowledgeable. Why? Probably because to be market-directed, the required infrastructure tends to prevent the problems we outlined earlier. The implication, then, is that converting to a market-directed perspective may be the most successful strategy executives and elected leadership can employ to avoid the negative impact of dismissal both on the executive and the association. A change in executive leadership is a highly costly event to any association that is not fully prepared for the transition.

Defining Success

In the organizations we studied, how three common issues were handled often made the difference between executives' success and failure. All three issues relate to the clarification and development of consensus of what constitutes success.

Whether the organization used process or outcomes as the basis of measuring success was significant. If they decided that success constituted following a specific process or plan that had been agreed to, then they were using process as the measurement. But if the organization clearly articulated the benefits it sought to achieve for its members and did so in the goals for its long-range plan, the objectives articulated in the business plan for each program, and in the performance appraisal process for each staff member, it was using outcomes as the measure. We found that where the measurement system focused on process rather than outcome, there was no significant contribution to helping define achievements that would benefit members.

We also found a major issue related to segmented needs. The primary concern was which segment's needs would serve as the basis for articulating the outcomes to be pursued. In successful organizations, a clear needs assessment process, with results honestly communicated through healthy channels, created a common understanding of the decision, if not agreement with it. There was clarity about the membership focus of the organization and tremendous sensitivity to the needs of members who were active participants.

And finally, we could not find a single instance of termination where a healthy consensus-building process was in place. What are the elements of a healthy process? A systemic needs assessment process that promotes agreement on the needs, wants, and expectations of the members. A strategic planning process that operates continuously at all levels of the organization, invites frequent review and adjustment, and is constantly informed by rational information about member needs, strategic position of the association, and evolving dynamics of the marketplace. A deliberative policy process that involves a series of decision steps informed by the perspective of both the staff and members that promotes rational decisions. The importance of the deliberative planning and policy process informed by committees, task forces, and staff expertise cannot be overemphasized. It tends to produce decisions that are not just acceptable, but are right. It also tends to produce confidence in the decisions themselves on the part of members. Even when members disagree with the judgments made, they have faith that the judgment is credible and based on rational information. The judgment is deemed legitimate.

Prevention Strategies

The results of this research have significant implications for the competencies successful association executives will demonstrate in the 21st century. Among them are three key prevention strategies that can be used by executives and volunteer leadership to avoid the costly effects of dismissal.

Confront and clarify expectations regularly and routinely. That includes expectations about role, about where on the continuum of staff driven to member driven the organization wants to be, and about what benefits will accrue to which member population. The days when a smile and an arm around the back at a nice cocktail party were enough to maintain comfort with management of operations are gone.

Focus time, communications, and resources on responsive outcomes for members.
Begin and end any discussion with the question, What will the results be for members? If you can't answer the question, you probably haven't finished the discussion. If you haven't answered the question in a satisfactory way, then you probably want to reassess what you are preparing to do.

Continually revitalize consensus-building mechanisms.
Make sure you have in place, employ, and constantly attend to a sound strategic planning process. Build it into every meeting of the board and make sure every committee is involved. Make sure that attention is constantly drawn to the most significant outcomes you are trying to achieve on the members' behalf. Ensure your needs assessment process builds a common data base that helps determine not just your members' opinions, but what it is that's causing those opinions. Define your policy process before you set policy. If you do not maintain the process, individuals who disagree with a decision will attack the process by which the decision was made, rather than argue against the decision itself. And be prepared to market intangibles when you unveil a public policy position or significant repositioning of power, norms, or values.

Learning how to execute behaviors that earn credibility, trust, and respect with today's diverse membership is critical to the success of 21st-century executives.

CHAPTER 4
Major Trends Affecting Associations

A multitude of trends, events, and occurrences affect associations today. Although differences exist in the combined effect these trends have on any given association, there are a few extraordinarily significant and dramatic trends emerging that, in combination with each other, are reshaping the context within which most associations will find themselves operating into the 21st century. This chapter will examine the most significant of these trends and explore their implications for the competencies that will be required by association executives.

The five interrelated trends are:
- a change in the nature of change itself;
- increased demand for outcome accountability;
- less time from talented volunteers;
- technology's promise, possibilities, expectations, and realities; and
- generational and multicultural demographics.

A Change in the Nature of Change Itself

There are two dimensions to this trend. The first is a significant escalation in the rate of change we are experiencing. The second is a significant alteration in how change manifests itself.

What do we mean by a change in the rate of change? We now have the ability to learn more about more things in greater depth

45

than we ever thought possible. This means that just when we believe that we have discovered the dynamic in any given situation, the nature of the situation itself tends to change.

There is a relationship between this rapid escalation in the rate of change and two primary characteristics 21st-century associations will need to exhibit. *The two primary characteristics are fluidity and flexibility.* For large associations especially, the implications are enormous because the systems and structures traditionally in place tend to be obstacles to fluidity and flexibility. In the 21st century, associations will need to respond to opportunities and problems more rapidly than ever before. The traditional governance approaches of most large associations (physically gathering a large group of members together to ensure participation on a broad base) will tend to inhibit the ability to serve members, rather than create opportunities to be responsive to them.

There is also a relationship between the rate of change and the second dimension of change—the alteration of how change manifests itself. Increasingly, significant change being experienced by associations is discontinuous rather than continuous change (Exhibit 5). In the past, a large portion of the change most important to us was predictable. We invested large amounts of time in developing trends and establishing assumptions based on these trends. Most trends were expected to exhibit a life cycle like an upward, predictable curve. In other words, we could predict the direction and outcome of a particular trend. We could create detailed long-range plans or road maps for the future, requiring only subtle modification as the future unfolded.

We now find ourselves in a period of time when change is much more rapid and much less continuous. Many associations will find large blocks of time invested in trend identification and detailed longrange forecasting will have less and less utility to their ability to do the right things at the right time.

Consider this example: The migration of capital to Eastern Europe to rebuild the infrastructure of East Germany after the fall of the Berlin Wall dramatically impacted the availability and cost of capital in the Western marketplace. America's business cycle, many economists tell us, remained in sluggish recovery for a longer time than usual as a result, at least in part, because of this phenomena. Many association members felt a financial crunch. Association budgets were then affected by their members' real or perceived financial condition. The point of the example is this: The impact of the Berlin Wall coming down, though historically positive, had an unforeseen and unpredicted impact on associations.

A larger portion of the most significant changes impacting associations are caused by events that are increasingly less predictable. The certainty of past predictable trend curves no longer exists. The graphic depiction of change today looks more like an electrocardiogram. It comprises of high peaks and low valleys occurring in more compressed time spans than ever experienced before.

Exhibit 5: Change in the Nature of Change Itself

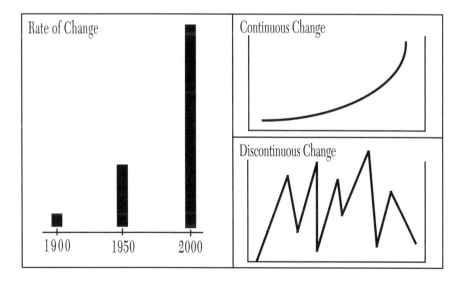

The information age has created a reality that makes enormous amounts of information from large groups of people more available to smaller groups of decision makers. This results in a greater number of intense decisions being made in greatly compressed time periods. This reality, in turn, has effected the nature of change itself, requiring associations to be more fluid, flexible, and responsive. Associations today have a variety of mechanisms available for continuously touching base with virtually every member of the organization. This provides the opportunity for associations to rethink the tradition of large governing bodies physically assembling in a single place for the purpose of exchanging experiences and opinions. New approaches to participatory decision making will significantly affect the competencies required of tomorrow's executive.

Increased Demand for Outcome Accountability

Driven by the changing nature of change itself, association members' marketplaces and professions are changing with greater rapidity and less predictability. The results are continually changing member needs and an increasingly diverse membership simultaneously demanding (a) greater focus on personal benefits and (b) greater outcome accountability of leaders.

In the past, members of associations tended to be satisfied with a comprehensive list of features of membership, i.e., the products and services available to them as a result of their membership. In today's environment, this is no longer adequate. Members expect direct benefits from membership—in fact, direct personal benefits. For example, a feature of membership is the availability of educational products. The member benefit is the opportunity to learn and acquire knowledge. The direct personal benefit is that this increased knowledge results in increased compensation, a promotion, or professional recognition.

The attendant consequence to associations is that it is no longer sufficient to be accountable for implementing a well-crafted, long-range plan. Members expect leaders to also be accountable for the direct personal benefits that are supposed to be received by them as a result of execution of the plan. In other words, they evaluate what the association is doing in terms of the benefit that accrues to them, rather than in terms of the actions of the association.

Perceived value is of critical importance. There are a variety of new competitors to associations and new places where member needs are being served. Competitors may be private vendors or public agencies, the member's employer, or cable television. Combine this with the fact that what is perceived as having value by members is becoming increasingly diverse, and there exists a greater challenge in earning member loyalty and commitment.

The number of segments of membership with differing views of what they believe constitutes the benefits they are looking for is rapidly growing. Member needs are evolving into three levels (Exhibit 6).

The first level is a need that is commonly shared by all segments of the membership. In any association, a segment may be defined as *a group of members who share similar psycho-demographic characteristics that make them definably different than another subgroup of members with different characteristics.* Variables of segmentation could be, for example, size of business, marketplace specialty or marketing approach, the age or educational level of the member and such. Each segmentation has implications for how members view themselves and their world. These views also influence what they expect from their association. *Level one needs are broad, common needs that all segments of the membership share.* Examples might be the need for a sense of professional identity, the need for a journal that represents that identity, or the need for educational programs and information.

The second level of need being increasingly exhibited by association members relates to delivery. *Within the broad, common*

Exhibit 6: Increased Demand for Outcome Accountability

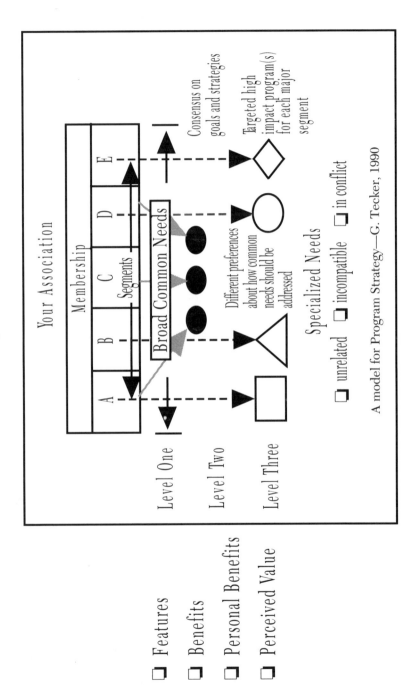

needs shared by all segments of the membership, there are significant differences in preference of how they want these needs met. For example, the full membership has a need for continuing education, a level one need. However, one segment of membership may prefer large meetings with expert speakers, while others prefer small, intimate, experiential learning opportunities, and still others want audiotapes for use in the car or computer-assisted learning opportunities. It is not just the benefit that the member is looking for, but the delivery system of the benefits they desire.

The third level need: rapidly emerging are entirely specialized needs: a need that one segment of the membership has that is specialized in nature and not shared by other member segments. Historically, when confronted with this situation, associations tended to spin off another association—or discover that another association had been spun off. However, inclusivity in this differentiated marketplace will be of strategic importance to many associations.

Inclusivity requires that programmatic strategies be employed to meet the specific and unique needs of each significant membership segment, while at the same time preserving focus on the common interests of the membership as a totality. Using member needs assessment data, associations can identify priority issues for each segment of the membership. By selecting one priority area for each segment—ensuring that no area selected is incompatible with any other area—an association can meet a specialized need of each segment while preserving the majority of its resources for use in meeting those needs commonly held by all members. By paying attention to priority needs of specialized member segments, tomorrow's association will be better able to preserve member loyalty within an increasingly diverse population. What is needed to understand and appreciate such complexity, and to devise and execute strategies to respond to it, has significant implications for the intellectual competencies of the 21st-century executive.

Less Time from Talented Volunteers

There appear to be two primary reasons why talented volunteers have less and less time to contribute to associations. First, the professional and personal lives of members are becoming more complicated. It is more difficult to balance personal and professional demands, resulting in less discretionary time for talented volunteers to contribute to the leadership of associations.

Second, there is more competition for the discretionary time of talented volunteers. There are more opportunities for involvement, and talented volunteers are becoming more selective in choosing opportunities that meet their personal needs and values. Talented volunteers are interested in the quality of the experience—the enjoyment and excitement of what they are doing—as much as they are interested in the altruistic or remunerative rewards that may come from an investment of personal time.

The declining availability of volunteer time has significant implications. Associations will need to find new ways to get work done, rather than asking members to reorganize their lives to fit traditional models of volunteer activity. These are likely to be work strategies that allow volunteers to assume smaller but more frequent "bytes" of the same apple. This should not be misconstrued as meaning these smaller units of work and responsibility will have less impact or importance. Rather, this is a human resource strategy that recognizes that not everyone, and especially not the most talented and, therefore, most in demand volunteer, has the time to effectively handle a responsibility with a large scope that must be maintained over a longer period of time. This means redesigning volunteer jobs and responsibilities to allow shorter term, high-impact assignments with tighter scope. Such a strategy will also contribute to an association's efforts to be more nimble by increasing fluidity, flexibility, and responsiveness.

Associations will also need to rely more heavily on outcome-oriented strategic plans to inspire involvement and guide individual activities. When talented volunteers agree to contribute time and energy, they expect to understand the broad purpose of their activities. It is also very likely that successful organizations will become more dependent on professional staff to execute work, responsive to specifications that have been constructed by member/staff task groups relying on the knowledge produced by comprehensive member needs assessments. This does not mean that membership will defer its involvement in direction setting, or that elected leadership will abrogate their responsibility to lead. It does mean that the nature of the partnership between paid and volunteer leadership will change to look more like an integrated team of peers, and less like the hierarchical relationship of employer and employee. The executive of the year 2000 will need to be very comfortable participating in leadership as a peer within a group. The bifurcated roles of employee of the board and boss of the staff and the very different behaviors often associated with each role, will be superseded by a more integrated role where behavior with members and staff is less schizophrenic.

Technology's Promise, Possibilities, Expectations and Realities

Computers, communications systems, and "softer" knowledge technologies are dramatically expanding the possibilities available to associations. The potential appears virtually unlimited. There are new ways of meeting without leaving home; new ways of getting work done together. The development of group decision-making software—groupware—is providing innovative ways of participative decision making in building solutions to complex problems. Expert systems software—smartware—provides increased comfort that judgments being made from data have a higher degree of certainty. Communications technology can allow instant access to the opinions, views, and experience of virtually every member of an association.

Members of most associations have increasingly higher expectations for their association's use of technology. Everyone wants to be on the leading edge and be able to use the information available to full advantage. The members of many associations, however, tend to be more willing to make more demands for technology than they are willing to invest in the systems required to meet those demands. Member competence in actually using that technology is far different in many associations than what members might voice as their desires or intents. As a result, the relationship of member views and the association's technologies often looks like this:

Exhibit 7: Technology's Promise

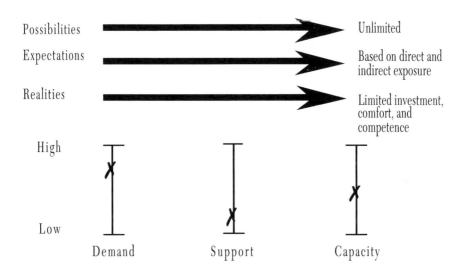

- **High demand** to take advantage of technology's promise
- **Medium capacity** to utilize the potential
- **Very low support** for paying for it.

This dilemma is often complicated by other technology-related concerns within the organization. Questions about the selection, design, implementation, and use of technology often raise uncomfortable questions about current practices or past history. (For example, an association may have made sound decisions about technological expansion in the past, but the speed of innovation has required that large investments in stand-alone systems be replaced with integrated systems of greater use and capacity.) Some leaders become paralyzed by the level of investment required for adequate technology. As a result, organizations best positioned to utilize these opportunities may be poorly positioned politically to move forward. One of the common elements that appears consistently within organizations overcoming this dilemma is the presence of a board member or group of board members who are considered knowledgeable and credible by their less technology experienced peers. This suggests that associations may be only as sophisticated about technology as their most sophisticated board member, since decision makers not yet comfortable or competent with technology will usually turn to a respected peer for guidance.

A 21st-century association making the commitment to be knowledge-based (as described in Chapter 2) will need to use information infrastructure as the artery that allows the necessary flow of knowledge to occur throughout the organization. *This emerging reality will pressure associations to expertly confront their technology dilemma with a coherent, longer range strategy of incremental*

Exhibit 8: Information Gap

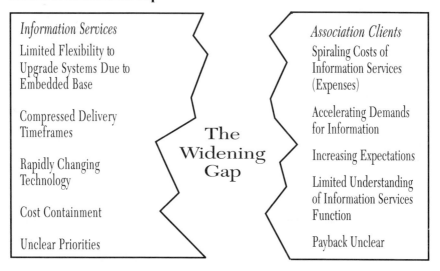

Information Services	The Widening Gap	Association Clients
Limited Flexibility to Upgrade Systems Due to Embedded Base		Spiraling Costs of Information Services (Expenses)
Compressed Delivery Timeframes		Accelerating Demands for Information
Rapidly Changing Technology		Increasing Expectations
Cost Containment		Limited Understanding of Information Services Function
Unclear Priorities		Payback Unclear

growth toward the possible use of integrated technology that may not even be known today. The need to take advantage of today's products will have to be balanced against concern about investing in soon obsolete systems. Many associations will need to take reasonable steps forward. They will need to move toward a technology vision based on use rather than system, employing evolution-friendly hardware and software systems to the extent possible.

Generational and Multicultural Diversity

The homogeneous membership of many associations is giving way to a membership reflecting increased generational and multicultural diversity. The particular combination of things that distinguish the needs and preferences of one member from the combination of things that distinguish the needs and preferences of another member are becoming more different than ever before (see Exhibit 9).

Exhibit 9: Generational and Multicultural Demographics

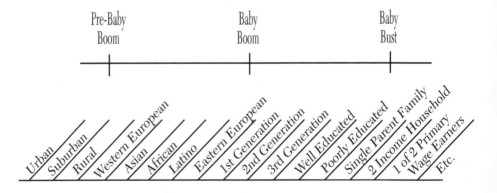

Generational diversity or multigenerationalism reflects the fact that it is likely most associations will have at least three distinct generations present in the membership in the 21st century. The three generations of adults currently active in association memberships are generally referred to as (a) the pre-boom, those born prior to 1945, (b) the baby boom, those born from 1945 to 1965, and (c) the post-boom, those born after 1965. Each of these generations have definably different views of the world, values, interests, and needs than the others. Each generation is actively making significantly different demands on an organization. Even when each generation is making similar demands in terms of the benefits they seek, they are often making different demands related to delivery system preferences and decision-making processes (see Exhibit 10).

Multicultural diversity is also growing within associations as a reflection of the growing diversity of our workplace and communities. Just as there are generational differences of expectations, values, and behaviors, there are also significant differences within multicultural groups. Leading effectively within an environment characterized by generational and multicultural diversity will be a significant challenge for many organizations into the 21st century. The response to that challenge will be characterized by fluidity, flexibility, and responsiveness. It will also require a fundamental respect for, and understanding of, the differences among members that this diversity represents. Successful associations will view these differences as a source of strength—not because of politeness or political correctness—but because the soundness of decisions and programs in an increasingly complex world will be enhanced by employing differentiated perspectives as tests to increase the probability that important decisions will be right and important activities will be supported.

Implications of the Trends Affecting Associations

To better understand the significance and implications of these trends, it is useful to establish a common understanding of the structure of an association as an enterprise. As complex organizations, an association structure could be displayed in a variety of ways. One such display, particularly useful in understanding the

Exhibit 10: Who We Are, What We're Like

Generation	Pre-Boomer (Over 55)	Baby Boomer (30s to 40s)	Baby Bust (teens to 20s)	Baby Boomlet (under 20)
Time-frame	— 1945 —	— 1964 —	— 1975 —	
Major Experiences	• World War II • Depression • Sacrifice • Hard work for a better future	• Prosperity & large size • Responsive marketplace & public policy • Crunched by its own size later	• Prosperity & smaller size • High tech/high touch • Competition with boomer for resources; activist on self-interest issues later	• Uncertain prosperity and larger size • Boomer and buster parents with active grandparents • High tech/high touch • Latch key phenomenon in 2 income families
Key Motivator	Stability & Security	Respect & Success	Enjoyable Experience	
Frequent Values	• Loyalty • Experience is the best teacher; "pay your dues" • Respect for authority & institutions	• High social conscience & self-interest (do good & do well) • Work as part of self-identity; credential important • Demand for involvement in decision-making • Hard work for institutions they feel appreciated by	• Self-indulgent; non-competitive • Not involved in issues • Work as a means to some unknown end; how time is spent more important than what is being done • Expectation of entitlement to good life • Little loyalty to institutions	
Major Psychographic subsegments	• Vitally active • Adapters • Overwhelmed	• Achievers/self-satisfied • Contented traditionalists • Discontented traditionalists • Hippies/neo-hippies	• Haves; well educated • Have nots; poorly educated	

anticipated paradigm shifts and their implications for executive competency, is presented in Exhibit 11.

In this model of infrastructure, not-for-profit organizations are visualized as comprising six basic structures enabled by four essential processes.

Exhibit 11: A Model of Association Infrastructure

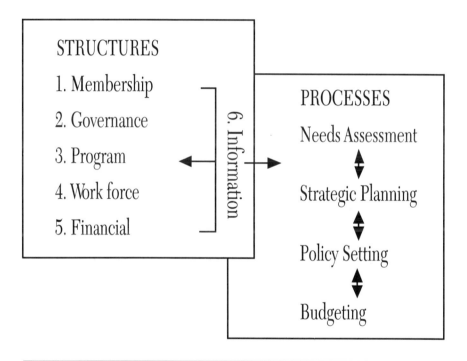

Membership Structure

The membership structure of an association involves who can be a member, how membership groups are classified and organized, and the rights and prerogatives enjoyed by various membership categories. Membership structure also includes the degree of intensity of involvement, or centralness to identity, exhibited by certain populations relevant to the association.

From another perspective, membership structure also involves understanding who are the organization's core members, members, customers, and key stakeholders.

Core members are individuals or groups without whom the fundamental character of the association would be altered. Several member segments can coexist as core membership, as long as they share common interests of sufficient importance and magnitude to supersede more specific interests that might differ. Core members expect that their association will never implement a program or policy that contradicts their interests. Core members also expect that programs and policies of the association will always support their interests. The mission of an association is usually focused on the common self-interests of its core membership. This does not imply, however, that associations cannot provide services to individuals who are not part of the core membership. Associations do provide benefits to populations external to the core, as long as the provision of those programs serves the interest of the core members.

Core members do not, by virtue of this designation, enjoy any opportunities or privileges of membership greater than any other member. The primary value of identifying the core membership within the general membership is to provide strategic focus to decisions related to program, policy, and resource decisions when choices are required.

Members are all individuals or groups eligible to belong to the association. Every core member is a member; but not every member is a core member. Individuals or groups that compose the core membership and any and all other individuals or groups who can join are members.

Customer refers to any individual or group either ineligible for membership or who chooses not to belong. Customers do not enjoy the rights and privileges of membership. They constitute specific populations who may wish to purchase access to the association's programs or services on a fee or subscription basis. For many associations, the identification and solicitation of customers may increasingly become a significant source of non-dues revenue. The potential political and income benefits of a strategy to servicing customers may also prompt many associations to consider collaboration with like-minded groups previously perceived as competitors. In either case, however, associations will need to ensure that access to programs and services granted to customers and the cost of promoting such access is in the real best interest of the membership, and does not actually diffuse resources better applied to directly serving the membership's needs.

Stakeholder refers to all individuals or groups who have a significant explicit or implicit interest in the activities or accomplishments of an association. They are often the interested targets of association communication, cooperation, or influence.

We anticipate significant shifts in the geographical boundaries that have historically served as the basis for many membership structures. Globalization, and distinguishable sets of self-interest unrelated to geography, will continue to alter traditional boundaries well into the 21st century.

Governance Structure

Governance structure refers to decision-making units of the organization and the relative powers, authorities, and responsibilities that each possesses. Governance structure also refers to the composition of each decision-making unit and how individuals are selected to participate in them.

The governance structures of associations vary widely. There are, however, some patterns that can be discerned. These patterns often typify trade associations, professional societies, and charitable and philanthropic groups.

Trade associations tend to resemble a more corporate model. They seek clarity in the chain of command and more centralized control for the purposes of effecting greater efficiency and definable accountabilities.

Professional societies tend to reflect more of a participatory or democratic structure. A greater number of larger bodies of people are involved more directly in a larger number of decisions. Many professional societies historically have tended to model themselves on a federal or political form of government. Expediency is often sacrificed to involvement to ensure that action taken has been approved by a majority of a group representative of various segments of membership.

Charitable or philanthropic organizations look more like professional societies than like trade associations. However, when their governing board is composed of representatives of a large number of local chapters or when the governing body has a significant fund-raising responsibility that parallels its responsibilities to govern, the distribution of powers and responsibilities tends to be different than either their professional or trade colleagues.

We anticipate that computer and communications technology and the softer technologies of market research will enable 21st-century organizations to more frequently capture the views of a greater number of members more directly. This will enable governance structures of future associations to find new ways to expedite decision making without sacrificing sensitivity or responsiveness to member opinions. These new methodologies in governance will have significant implications for the behaviors required of executives managing less representative but more knowledgeable decision-making processes.

Program Structure

The program structure of an association is composed of its business lines, programs within those business lines, and specific events or activities within programs. Program structure is the work of the association. Examples of business lines are government affairs, communications, education, technical standards, and such. An example of a program within a business line would be a series of interactive teleconferences on selected topics conducted as a part of the education business line. An example of specific activity would be the teleconference on emerging needs of our work force conducted as one event within the teleconference series program.

We anticipate that (a) increased segmentation of membership subpopulations, and (b) increasing diversity in member preferences for delivery systems to meet a growing, wider range of needs will have significant implications for the program structures of 21st-century associations. The executives of those associations will re-quire a high degree of competence in understanding complex rela-tionships to effectively facilitate planning decisions and manage the program delivery systems of tomorrow's associations.

Work Force Structure

Work force structure refers to an association human resource pool, both volunteer and employed. The organization's committee sys-tem, staff divisions or departments, and relationships with outside experts and contractors constitute the work force of most associa-tions. To maintain nimbleness, minimize down time, increase pro-ductivity, and most effectively leverage available assets, many orga-nizations are shrinking their full-time, permanent care of their work force. In exchange, they are expanding partnerships and alliances with temporary and specialized experts and workers whose specific contributions can be purchased and cost-effectively targeted as particular needs arise.

We anticipate that the rate of change in the larger world of which members are a part will require tomorrow's associations to exhibit a significantly higher degree of responsiveness, flexibility, and fluidity in work force structure. This will be increasingly important for any association to be able to quickly refocus its assets on a rapidly evolving and frequently shifting set of priorities. The communica-tion skills needed to ensure consistency of direction and coherency of program in such a rapidly changing organizational environment will be prerequisites for success in the 21st century.

Financial Structure

The financial structure of an association includes the sources of its revenue, the relative proportion of revenue from various sources, the allocation and placement of available revenue, and the anticipated cost of resources and opportunities over time. Dues structures, investment strategies, and projected estimates of significant costs anticipated into the foreseeable future are examples of considerations related to financial structure. Basic decisions related to the fiscal status of an organization (for example, for-profit or not-for-profit) and decisions related to the selection of tax-exempt status (for example 501C3 vs. 501C6) are determinations about financial structure with enormous strategic implications. A growing number associations are considering parallel or subsidiary organizations that may or may not replicate the financial structure of the parent or sibling organization. Financial structure is increasingly being viewed as a strategic alternative. A specific structure is selected by the association at a given point in time because it is, or will, provide a significant strategic advantage to the organization's ability to effectively service its members.

We anticipate that 21st-century executives will need sophisticated skills in acquiring and using specialized information to effectively consider the strategic implications of financial structures in a rapidly paced marketplace. We also believe interpersonal skills, especially those related to the management of group process, will be essential to facilitating groups working with a sometimes unpredictably shifting spectrum of resource allocation decisions with complex technical and political implications.

Information Structure

Information structure links the previously discussed five elements to each other. It also links the structures of an association to its basic decision-making processes. The information structure must ensure that individuals and groups executing activity in each of the other five elements of structure have the data, information, and knowledge they require to make sound decisions and effectively execute work.

Information structure includes (a) the decisions that will be needed at each and all levels of the organization; (b) the data and information that will be required to effectively make those decisions; (c) the sources of the data and information that will be needed; (d) the systems for collecting the requisite information from appropriate sources; (e) the methods for tabulation and analysis that aggregate and categorize the data and information; and (f) the hardware, software, systems, and processes that will be used to interpret the information, integrate it with the appropriate know how and systematically distribute or provide access to it in useful forms to the persons or places that will need to make or coordinate judgments based on it.

We anticipate that a new set of competencies related to interaction with information will be required of executives to function effectively in the 21st century. Much of the future nature, organization, manipulation, and application of information that will be potentially relevant to association executives is still unknown. Skills related to learning to use various kinds of information in a variety of forms and ways that may not as yet even be conceived will be a highly valued executive competency of tomorrow.

The Four Processes

Four processes, linked to the six elements of structure by information, serve as the primary conduits through which knowledge is translated into decisions. These four basic processes for decision making in associations include needs assessment; strategic planning; policy setting; and budgeting.

Effective *needs assessment* involves a variety of data collection methodologies employed in a coherent strategy to continuously collect and interpret information about membership, program, and the larger world within which members are functioning. Needs assessment can include activities such as written, electronic, or telephone survey; personal or telephone interviews; focus group research; assessment of member behavior by analysis of an accurate behavioral data base; and a variety of other market research-like technologies.

Successful *strategic planning* involves a continuous process of thoughtfully determining direction, at all levels of the organization, on the basis of careful assessment of present and future conditions relative to achievement of clearly defined and desired outcomes. The strategic planning process of the most effective associations usually include a variety of activities undertaken through each of the basic phases of (a) data collection; (b) direction setting; (c) strategy development for programs, organization structure and process, finance, technology, and the like; (d) action planning to guide implementation and accountability; and (e) monitoring and adjustment as events in the larger world, new information, or experience in implementing strategy suggest the need for change.

Effective *policy setting* in most associations involves established and clear procedures for rational deliberation. It defines the intellectual and political steps participants take to produce judgments related to (a) positions the organization takes on public issues of importance to the membership or (b) statements of direction, guidelines, or parameters established as frameworks within which operations are to be executed. Successful policy systems most often also include systematic procedures for maintaining written, easily accessible documentation of policy determinations made by all units of the organization with policy-level authority.

A successful *budgeting process* in most associations includes a systematic analysis of needs, opportunities, and capacity. This analysis produces a fiscal manifestation of the organization's program plan. In the absence of a strategic, program, or business plan, an association's budgeting process will often become, by default, the only process available for determining programs and priorities. This often produces politicized program and policy decisions driven by money available rather than by strategically important member needs.

We anticipate that these four basic decision-making processes will undergo dramatic changes in 21st-century associations. The interaction of structure and process in successful associations will alter to respond to significant shifts in the dynamics of the larger world within which they operate. They will significantly modify the dynamics of the organization to better fit new environmental requirements. As the dynamics of the organization evolve, the fullness and focus of an executive's portfolio of professional competencies will also need to evolve accordingly.

New Dimensions in Essential Executive Competencies

The specific trends and combination of phenomena, which may affect any one association, will be unique and peculiar to that organization. The particular dynamics of any industry, profession, or issue arena will create a somewhat customized "issues landscape" for any given association. There are some shifts, however, that are fundamental and common to many associations. These shifts, we believe, can be anticipated to significantly alter the character of many not-for-profit organizations.

The following summaries do not reflect all of the implications of these shifts for any association or executive nor do they fully represent all the trends and emerging realities that suggest their importance. They do serve, however, as a useful synopsis of what many associations expect. These changes in organizational character have profound implications for the portfolio of competencies that will be exhibited by successful executives into the 21st century.

From Territorial to Global

Changes in (a) traditional market segments, (b) interdependent economies, and (c) expanding international opportunities suggest there will be significant change in the geographic parameters that have historically defined the interests, membership, and organizational structure of many associations.

From Enforcer to Consultant

Expanding member needs for usable knowledge, increasing diversity in the larger world and the membership, and member demand for a greater return on investment suggest there will be significant change in the roles many associations fill for their members and how many associations interact with their subparts. Associations will need to redirect energy from enforcing the rules of membership (especially with chapters or sections) to assisting members (and subunits of membership) to accomplish desired outcomes.

From Political Oligarchy to Market Directed

An increasingly complex marketplace and workplace and an increasingly diversifying membership suggest there will be a need for decision-making at all levels of many associations to be based more on defensible research about the membership and their world. The well-intended views of a relatively small number of officials, developed in a decision-making environment that is opinion rich, but information poor, will be an increasingly insufficient knowledge base.

From Compromise to Synergy

The growing need to achieve demonstrable results on an increasingly diverse set of member needs and the increasing importance of maintaining consensus about what will constitute success within a frequently changing environment suggest there will be a need for many associations to reach consensus by determining how commonly desired outcomes can best be achieved. The more traditional political approach of seeking the lowest common denominator acceptable to everyone will be increasingly ineffective.

From Uniformity to Inclusive with Segments

Diversification of the marketplace, work force, community, and membership and the rate and amount of increasingly unpredictable change suggest there will be a need for significant alteration of programming philosophy in many associations. Large initiatives with diffused relevance to any particular group will become increasingly less attractive in many associations. Increased sophistication in meeting the targeted needs of a wider variety of groups with differentiated program content and delivery systems will be needed. Fewer programs of higher value to more targeted populations will be used as a program strategy to maintain defensible niches in a world of increased choices.

From Mass to Customized

Increased segmentation, rapidity of change, and member demand for value from their investment suggest many associations will need to become more capable of converting their collective resources into a customizable capacity. The organization will need to function as a pool of resources from which can be ordered specialized programs, service, and information support focused on the specific real needs of a user.

From an Inner Directed Business to an Outer Directed Business

Increased demand to focus the resources of the organization on achieving results and greater intolerance of internal political agendas and bureaucracy suggest there will be a need in many associations to redirect attention from internal affairs to the work that must be accomplished. As associations become more involved in meeting the real needs of their members, they are likely to become more influential in effecting the dynamics of the industry, profession, or issues area that they serve. In turn, the association that becomes a player within its arena of interest, will become increasingly attractive to and appreciated by its member constituents.

These seven fundamental shifts in the paradigm of many associations have powerful implications for not-for-profit enterprises into the 21st century. Most associations can reasonably anticipate an evolving infrastructure. Each of these anticipated shifts will have dramatic and multiple impact on the six basic elements of structure and the four key decision-making processes of associations.

The new realities confronting association executives in the next century will be driven by such paradigm shifts. The competencies in this study have been identified as essential to a 21st-century executive's professional attributes.

These professional attributes assume special significance because of the profound changes these powerful shifts in organizational personality imply for so many associations. They do not represent a replacement for current competencies or even a deemphasis of the importance of more traditional knowledge about association management. They do represent the next dimension of professionalism that is becoming as important as all we have learned before.

SECTION II

The Competencies

CHAPTER 5
The Competencies of
21st-Century Leadership

The description of leadership competencies found on the following pages is not intended to replace or supersede existing definitions of executive behavior. It is intended to expand on them—to create a new dimension or understanding of the subtle difference between a competent executive and a competent executive leader in the 21st century. For the most part, these subtle differences are not easily measured quantitatively. They are qualitative and complexly interrelated attributes and behaviors. Competencies are being developed and exhibited in response to a rapid shifting in the external and internal organizational environment of associations.

Though our research and conclusions are focused on the association executive, we strongly suspect that these competencies will be critical to the private, public, and charitable sectors, as well.

To provide a framework for our research and conclusions, we turned first to *A Scans Report for America 2000: Learning a Living: A Blueprint for High Performance,* published by the U.S. Department of Labor in April 1992. This report "describes the economic choices facing the United States, defines the workforce issues as presently understood, and makes recommendations to set the nation on the path to a high-performance future." Imbedded in this report is an excellent categorization of the competency areas required in the workplace of the future: resources, interpersonal skills, information, systems, and technology. The specific substantive competencies our research identified as germane to association executives were assigned to the Scans categories. (An invitation extended in the federally sponsored report to all industries, occupations, and professions.) These executive competency areas are built on a foundation of basic skills and personal qualities.

Research Methodology

Drawing from over 600 case study files of existing associations, we used the Scans framework of five essential areas to categorize and define effective execution of critical competencies at the executive leadership level. These conclusions were tested and validated through group discussion and interaction with the competencies with hundreds of association executives in general learning opportunities intended to benefit both the participants and the research. In-depth interviews were conducted with over a dozen individuals identified by the research team as effective and forward-thinking executives who exhibited mastery in one or more of the competency areas.

The results have been further refined and supplemented with anecdotal material to enlighten and bring to life the competencies in action and to illustrate the resulting reality when the competencies are poorly applied or not applied at all.

These illustrations represent composite portraits created by combining information from several sources and cases. If they appear very similar to any particular situation known to the reader, it is because they are reflective of realities many people experienced.

The Competency Definitions

In the broadest sense, we have defined the executive leadership competencies of the 21st century as follows:

- **Interpersonal Skills:** The ability to work as an effective member of a group; teach others, listen, serve, lead, follow, negotiate, and work well with people from diverse cultural backgrounds.

- **Understanding Complex Relationships:** The ability to understand social, organizational, and technological systems and their interrelationships. The ability to evaluate and monitor progress. The ability to dynamically redesign structures and processes.

- **Acquiring and Using Information:** The ability to acquire, evaluate, organize, and interpret information, and communicate it in a way that is understood and relevant.

- **Valuing and Using Technology:** The ability to integrate information, knowledge, capacity, technological tools, and process to effectively achieve desired purposes.

- **Deployment of Resources:** The ability to prioritize and allocate time, money, materials, space, volunteer, and staff resources for maximum impact toward outcome achievement.

The competency definitions are themselves strongly interrelated one to another. Reduced to their simplest form, they revolve around relationships and knowledge: relationships among people, relationships among actions, relationships among resources, and effectively converting information into the knowledge required to support these relationships.

The association executive of the 21st century will be managing—in many ways is already managing—an organic organization and process. Gone are the days of compartmentalization, product-driven decisions, predictable change, using the past as a source of knowledge or standard of measure, and management by control. Today and tomorrow are focused on interdependence, cooperation, customization, involvement, and quality as defined and evaluated by the consumer—the members of the association. Executives are constantly dealing with the unknown, the unpredictable, searching for opportunities embedded in this ever changing landscape. Their standards of performance are defined by future needs.

Personal Characteristics

As we worked closely with the competencies and attributes detailed in the ensuing chapters, personal characteristics common to all of the competency areas began to emerge:

- Cooperatively builds, effectively articulates, and is focused on the vision of what success will look like.
- Cultivates and trusts instinct and intuition.
- Is opportunistic—what is emerging that might be turned to advantage?
- Is willing to risk success without assured outcomes.
- Has a holistic, multidimensional perception of the interdependence of people, actions, and resources.
- Inspires and serves others by providing the tools they need, creating a supportive environment for creative expression and risk taking.
- Trusts self and others, is open and vulnerable, and speaks with integrity.

Vision

Though it is much easier and more comfortable to talk about how to do something or the detail aspect of decisions, effective executives understand that the success of the organization hinges most critically on the ability of the group to articulate what success will look like when it is achieved. This must be done in concrete, descriptive outcome terms. For example, it does not mean stating that the association will advocate for the interests of members. The concrete descriptive outcome desired might be that government regulations create an environment of free trade for all members.

The effective leader knows that in order for people to support the goals of an organization these goals must be inspiring, far reaching and tangible—something that the members, staff and volunteer leaders of the organization can see and reach for in all of their actions. This is especially critical in a time of rapid change that requires responsiveness and flexibility. We no longer have the luxury, as leaders, to instruct people on how to contribute to organizational goals. We must build understanding and ownership of the goals within people, so that as factors change each individual is free to, and capable of, adjusting their activities and their contributions to stay on a course directed toward goal achievement. This is done by continually using the outcomes in all verbal and written communications and decision processes, so that they become firmly rooted in the organization—like the landing lights at an airport, guiding planes from all directions into the same destination and a smooth landing.

Intuition

Beyond the old notion of woman's intuition, the cultivation and trust of instinct and intuition is emerging as one of the subtle differences shared by effective executives of both genders. Intuition is a combination of the sum total of direct personal experience and an inner voice to be heard within. Some have termed it knowingness because it is the experience of knowing something without quantitative or physical evidence. In order to experience this knowingness, we turn our attention from exclusively outer-oriented—that which can be substantiated—and also listen for guidance on the inside. In fact, in the words of one executive, "intuition is the first part, not the last part of the creative or decision-making process. The outside resources and realities become vehicles for focusing the intuition—not the other way around." This requires the ability to notice and acknowledge feelings. It also requires periodic stillness and reflection. Acting on intuition especially requires self-trust and a willingness to sometimes act without documentable data or evidence.

Opportunity

One of the applications of both vision and intuition continually referenced by successful executives we interviewed and substantiated

by our consideration of the cases studied is the act of being opportunistic (not to be confused with opportunism or the act of seeking
personal gain at the expense of others). To be opportunistic is to
continually ask the questions, What is emerging from this changing
environment that can be turned to advantage in support of our
vision? What is trying to happen here that we have not noticed yet?
Opportunistic action is less involved in pushing or making
things happen and far more involved in uncovering, unfolding, and
bringing into brilliance that which is naturally trying to emerge
or occur. This is resource, or could we say energy conservation
at its best. It takes far less energy, and resources to uncover and
shine up something that occurs naturally than it does to create
something and make it happen from scratch. Most effective leaders
rarely start from scratch.

Willingness to Risk Success

Effective leaders in all types of situations and conditions demonstrate a profound willingness to risk success. They stretch both
the boundaries of their imaginations and trust to reach further
for peak achievements. In so doing, they accept the inevitable
reality that when you widen your, and your organization's range of
behavior, you also increase the likelihood of missteps or miscues. In
other words, effective leaders are willing to view these mistakes as
subservient occurrences that can be adjusted and fine-tuned along
the way, rather than as irrefutable signs of problems or poor
performance.

The challenge is to eliminate fear from the organization and to
create an environment in which it is safe to take risks. This usually
is accomplished by shifting from a system of judging people to a
system of evaluating the processes being used. It means replacing
punishment and disincentives in the workplace with rewards and
incentives that are meaningful to people and natural in the kind
of work being accomplished.

Holistic, Multidimensional Perspective

Effective executives view the organization holistically, and understand that doing less can mean being more, both personally and organizationally. The interdependence of people, actions, and resources has become an increasingly crucial leadership insight and competency as we move into an age of doing more with far less. It is also the key to doing less and being more as an organization.

Associations can no longer be viewed as compartmentalized pieces of a puzzle assembled under the umbrella of a common name. Within the most progressive organizations, departments are disappearing, being replaced by project work teams; committees are being replaced by ad hoc task groups; and line item budgets are being replaced by financial allocations linked to vision and outcome-oriented goals and objectives pursued with a strategic plan.

Service to Others

Echoing the popular concept of the "Servant Leader," many interviewees spoke candidly of the importance of operating from a service point of view. Not just service to members, but equally as important is service to those who are responsible for getting the work done. There was a strong quality of generosity in the comments and observations of these leaders as they spoke of giving freely of time—to listen and to coach—and of asking questions like, What do you need in order to get the job done? and then providing what is asked for. Their comments depicted a helpmate offering time, guidance, and support—not a supervisor offering instruction, control, and enforcement.

Trust and Openness

Implied in each of the competency areas is a fundamental trust in the good intentions and wisdom of individuals and groups of people. The very nature of associations, a place where like-minded people come together to achieve common goals within the world they live in, requires a high value on democratic process and the value of the individual, as well as a high degree of participation in decision-making by members and staff alike. This challenges the effective association leader to develop a fundamental trust in the discernment and capacity of others, a willingness to trust that group decisions based on collective knowledge and cooperatively reached are the best decisions for the association.

It also challenges the leader to be congruent in words and actions in order to earn the trust of members, volunteer leaders, and staff. For example, executives do not earn trust by saying that they seek diverse input from others or that they support others in stretching to risk success and then respond to uncomfortable feedback or mistakes by subtly or not so subtly punishing transgressors. Building an emotionally safe environment is a critically important task of the 21st-century leader.

Interviews with executives successful in executing the 21st-century competencies suggest that the most effective way to do this is to become vulnerable, open, and honest in the expression of true personal feelings as a leader. If the leader exhibits self-protective behavior, others in the organization will model this, as well. However, if the leader models a willingness and comfort with admitting mistakes or confusion, this will be tremendously empowering for others. From the perspective of one interviewee:

> The leader must be vulnerable. Employees are generally uncomfortable reporting screw-ups. But if they are in an environment where this happens at all levels, where they are able to share the truth and receive respect, not wrath, then the leader has the opportunity to assist in solving the problem or adjusting the process. If we spend half our energy covering up, then there is only half our energy remaining for action and accomplishment.

Self-Esteem and Self-Development

The picture that emerges from this list of attributes is one of a personally secure and centered individual, at once scanning the environment for unseen opportunities to support the vision and goals of the organization while providing an environment of trust, openness, personal safety, and nurturing within the organization.

Many of the executives interviewed spoke of the importance of an additional critical behavior: an insatiable curiosity and desire to learn. This valuing of knowledge was also a common character trait of executives identified in the case studies as having demonstrated competence in multiple situations. One interviewee summed it up by saying,

> I view the work environment as a tool for self-fulfillment and self-development. This is not incompatible with results. Getting in touch with who I am and being myself is vital to my well-being and my performance. When I allow myself and my coworkers the freedom to apply our passion to others' needs, the freedom to make our own contributions, then others, automatically benefit. If growth and learning are valued for all, then the organization must be successful. If personal growth stops, so will the organization's growth...

A significant number of executives also give equal emphasis to the importance of integrating a spiritual dimension into their leadership. This emerged as a deep faith and trust in a natural order of things and a desire to integrate spirituality into interpersonal relationships. In each case, executives identified the importance of introspection, self-investigation, a willingness to see themselves as they really are—what they can impact and what is beyond their sphere of influence—and a generous degree of self-acceptance and self-trust. When one executive was asked how he had developed a comfort with the leadership competencies described in this and the following chapters, his response was immediate and succinct: "Through dedicated self-investigation and experiential experimentation—I had to look inside in order to be effective outside."

CHAPTER 6
Interpersonal Skills

Interpersonal Skills: A Definition

The ability to work as a member of a group; teach others, listen, serve members, lead/follow, negotiate, and work well with people from culturally diverse backgrounds.

Interpersonal skills have long been touted as important to executive success. There are, however, several societal factors that are emphasizing the importance of these skills and broadening the competencies required to effectively exercise them. Among these factors is the increasing cultural diversity of both the work force and the membership of our associations. Multicultural diversity adds a new dimension to interpersonal relationships as it heightens the need for a respect and valuing of differences among people, as well as adding the need to be multiculturally literate. In other words, it is no longer enough to be tolerant of differences. It is essential that executives of the 21st century be well versed in the unique characteristics, practices, language, and norms of the diverse cultures represented within their environment.

A second factor increasing the importance of interpersonal skills is the increasing sense of isolation being experienced generally among people. As society becomes more fragmented and complex, individuals experience a craving for connection and sense of community. This craving often seeks fulfillment in the workplace and within associations. Executives are being asked, in fact required, to develop an ability to communicate—to truly hear and understand the needs and feelings of others in a more expansive and intimate way.

The third major factor is the increasing demand for participative decision making and consensus building. For any number of reasons, not the least of which is the maturing of the baby boom generation and its natural ascent to leadership positions, there is a much increased expectation that major decisions about direction and focus will be made in a participative manner at the very time that issues are growing rapidly more complex and response time is at a premium. This means that the executive of the 21st century will be required to expand beyond the traditional model of seeking input from others to make decisions, to an evolving model that will facilitate special interest or stakeholder groups speaking directly with each other and formulating decisions as a group.

The significance of these factors is dramatically heightened by the fact that associations and association leadership are first and foremost a group process. The association executive is responsible for building effective relationships with the board of directors and other volunteer leaders, the staff and the membership, as well as often being responsible for maintaining relationships with external stakeholders or publics. She or he is also a critical linchpin in the maintenance of healthy and dynamic relationships among and between these groups as well.

In our interviews with executives who served as effective executors of these competencies, the interpersonal competency area was consistently rated top priority. Let's take a look at what the specific competencies are emerging to be:

Key Competencies

- Recognizes, respects, values, and supports differences of personal style, opinion, and culture.

- Facilitates understanding and resolution of differences; builds consensus among diverse groups.
- Clearly communicates true feelings and thoughts with compassion and forthrightness; is able to *hear and understand* others.
- Translates understanding of the needs of others (including member needs) into positive actions to meet these needs.
- Questions, observes, and discerns issues and choices without judgment.
- Is open, receptive, and willing to take personal risk by communicating own vulnerabilities and fallibility.
- Supports and enhances the strengths of others
- Is congruent in words and actions.

This set of competencies is a far cry from the tough, invulnerable, take charge image of a leader of the past. Or in its more negative appearance, the leader who believed he or she must manipulate people into agreement, control all decision processes, and appear infallible to others, thereby engaging in indirect and fragmenting communications and often leading by intimidation. The successful 21st-century association executive will be a facilitator, coach, and mentor, not a battle commander.

Valuing Differences

Valuing differences is very different from tolerating differences. Recognizing, respecting, valuing, and supporting differences of personal style, opinion, and culture requires a release of the notion that there is a right way to be or do something. It is a belief that the workplace and our associations are enriched by a diversity of unique behaviors, opinions, and cultures. As one executive described, "It is no longer enough to make it OK to be different. We must make it desirable. We must 'celebrate' the differences within our organization. This requires self-acceptance which then can lead to mutual acceptance."

A 21st-century executive seeking to expand this competency will benefit from development training in multicultural literacy (i.e. studying the unique features of other cultures), as well as training in managing diversity (i.e. what are the techniques and approaches required to redesign your organization's culture to be multiculturally friendly). As some leaders have learned the hard way, creating a climate of diversity is not simply a matter of saying "We welcome those who are different." It is necessary to redesign communications and systems to demonstrate this commitment in visible and consistent ways.

The Leader as Facilitator: Building Consensus

Diversity of style, opinion, and culture brings with it special challenges for decision making and consensus building. How many times have you as a leader or part of a leadership group taken special care to seek the input of diverse groups within the organization before making a decision? But when you have taken this decision, carefully crafted to meet the needs of as many people as possible, back to the group, you have been met not with the appreciation and enthusiasm you had hoped for but with disappointment and perhaps even anger. Our experience and examination of the case studies indicate a major reason this happens is because there was no mechanism in this process for the diverse groups to hear and understand each other's point of view. There was no opportunity for competing interests to look each other in the eye and be accountable to each other.

Another reason is that the solution, the final decision, does not look like the requests or input that any group provided. The decision is usually a synthesis of many different ideas and needs and, therefore, even though you have acquired input from many, no one feels that they were really heard or understood in the final decision. This reality is occurring more often than in the past because of the growing diversification of your membership or work force.

Also relevant here are generational demographics. The baby boom generation, generally accepted as those born from 1945 to 1965, represents the largest generation in history, and likely represents a large percentage of your membership and work force. An identifiable characteristic of this generation is that it prefers not to give its authority to others. Most baby boomers prefer to participate in decision making. They tend to not trust or value representative governance in the same way previous generations were willing to delegate power. The do not, therefore, easily buy in to or support decisions made by a few.

This dynamic is further complicated by the need for widespread support and actions by many in the implementation of sound decisions. Absence of buy-in is no problem if we need only count on our own actions to achieve the desired goal. But in associations, we are usually dependent on the support and actions of many to achieve desired results. *Concensus based on synergy rather than compromise has become critically important to the success of associations.*

Effective consensus is built through facilitation. It is not a process of making a decision and then persuading others of its validity. It is a challenging process that involves bringing a group of people together—representatives of all of the major stakeholder positions within the group and providing the opportunity for the group to hear and understand each other's point of view. Out of this exchange the leader identifies and builds support for the common agreement that exists within the group. He or she also helps the group identify the impact of achieving one group's desires that may occur at the expense of others. For consensus building to be truly effective, the leader must elicit a commitment from participants that the "price of admission" to the group decision-making process is a willingness to hold yourself accountable for the effect of individual preferences and desires on others.

The significance of this increasingly, necessary consensus-building model to the competencies required of 21st-century executives is enormous. It requires the executive to possess extraordinary communications skills, and the ability to be a clear mirror, reflecting the group's opinions back to them in synthesized form without judgment. The 21st-century executive will be able to let go of the need to control the direction of discussion or the outcome, and learn to use key questions and observations to hold the group's focus to (a) the mission or purpose of the discussion and (b) the resource realities within which decisions are being made. The executive operates from discernment and helps the group to do the same; tomorrow's executive does not merely operate from personal judgment of what is right and wrong.

The desired outcome of such a process is a clear articulation of a direction, policy, or decision cooperatively reached. The leader's task then becomes assisting others to identify the contributions or actions each is willing to make to achieve the outcome or live within the decision.

Hearing and Understanding

One executive interviewed spoke specifically of his behavior in meetings:

> Criteria for the meeting is important. I ask that everyone use ownership language. That is 'I' statements such as I think..., I feel..., for me... It is also important that we agree that there is no stupid or invalid idea, need, or opinion. We may choose one idea or opinion over others based on the particular circumstance or issue, but this does not in any way invalidate the others not chosen. We also agree to frequently acknowledge each individual's contribution. One especially effective way is perception checking, verifying that what you think you have heard is what was in fact intended. This is done by saying, 'What I think I heard you say is...' and allowing the other person to correct

misperceptions. Then, rather than immediately proceeding to add an opinion, open-ended questions can be asked for clarification and building on the idea. In this way, participants are validated and all contributions are treated with respect.

Another executive spoke of his consensus-building and communications role this way:

> There is far more to consensus building and communication than just mustering a vote. The chief reason for my success is that I help the members learn to deal with each other. I listen to them closely, validate what I think I have heard, and summarize the desired outcomes I have heard them articulate. Then I link everything I say and do to this outcome, especially communication around spending.
>
> I also urge them to talk to each other. So often, various tribes complain to each other, but there is very little truth-telling. I encourage them and help them to tell the truth to each other.
>
> Now I am working with staff to teach them how to do this, to anticipate areas of disagreement and facilitate discussion and consensus. We are reconceptualizing staff roles; moving them from passive observer to active facilitator; filling in the gaps and making connections, linkages, among other parts of the association.

Translating Understanding Into Action

Hearing and understanding the needs of others is one part of the complex equation of effectiveness. Positive and congruent action is an equally important part of this equation. The effective 21st-century executive will invest heavily, for instance, in truly understanding the desires and needs of the membership. Based on this understanding the executive will seek to fulfill these needs as they are stated, not based only on what he or she thinks is really needed. The executive will also take every opportunity to relate the stated desires and needs to the actions being taken, linking in members' minds the request and the response.

The capability to translate understanding into action is one of the clearest points of confluence among the five arenas of 21st-century competency; it is also a significant place of confluence between 21st-century organizational culture and operations and the competencies of the executives leading them.

Enhancing the Strengths of Others

Individual performance evaluation and judgment are slowly being replaced by more continuous formative evaluation of the work processes being used and the results being achieved by the process. This allows the executive to more than merely summatively judge the performance of an individual. It promotes focus on the strengths of the individual, whether volunteer leader or staff member. The executive of the 21st century will become an advocate for individuals as he or she looks for the strength in each and supports the application and emergence of that strength for the mutual benefits of both the individual's fulfillment and the organization's success.

This also implies that 21st-century executives will not invest significantly in correcting their own weaker areas, but rather will continually seek to expand the use of their own personal strengths, while surrounding themselves with individuals who have strengths in the areas in which they are less talented. As one executive sees it, "It is about creating an environment in which the things each of us does best can come forth for the benefit of the organization. We are not about focusing on deficiencies, we are about focusing on strengths."

"Walking the Talk"

Employees and members have a highly developed ability to spot "BS." It is becoming increasingly critical that executives "walk their talk" in order to earn trust, respect, and credibility in relationships. In fact, one of the primary reasons for the downfall of programs such as Total Quality Management is the failure of top management to be congruent in words and action. Words like partnership, consensus, empowerment, member responsive, service, or quality are little more than slogans if they are not backed by the observable action of the executive. Such actions include where we spend our time, how we spend our money, when we reward, and even when our eyes light up with passion and enthusiasm as we interact with others.

What Happens in the Absence of Effective Execution of These Competencies

One likelihood is the perception or reality of manipulation. This is a complex and sensitive area. People are different, and will have different levels of need to process relationship issues or establish articulated commonness of values. Historically, the Western workplace has tended to place more value and reward on thinking and working styles that are extroverted (more so than introverted), sensing (more so than intuitive), thinking (more so than feeling), and judging (more so than perceiving).

Such preferences have been described by popular style inventories like the Myers Briggs Type Indicator. Using the Myers Briggs descriptions as a base, these preferences can be summarized.

Dimensions of Style

Extroversion–Introversion are complementary attitudes toward the world.

Extroverts are stimulated by their environment—the outer world of people and things. They are often friendly, talkative, and easy to know. They need relationships and easily express emotion. They feel pulled outward by external claims and conditions. They are energized by other people and external experiences. They act first, then (maybe) reflect. Extroverts give breadth to life.

An introvert's essential stimulation is from within—the inner world of thoughts and reflection. Introverts often seem reserved, quiet, and feel pushed inward by external claims and intrusions, but energized by inner resources and internal experiences. They reflect, then (maybe) act. Introverts give depth to life.

Sensing-Intuition are ways of taking in information.
The sensing person takes in information by way of five senses— seeing, hearing, smelling, touching, and tasting. They look at specific parts and pieces. They live in the present, enjoying what's here. Sensors prefer to handle practical matters. They like things that are definite and measurable. They start at the beginning and take one step at a time. They like to work hands-on with the parts, to see the overall design. Sensors prefer set procedures and established routines.

The intuition person processes information by way of an additional "sixth sense" or hunch. Intuitives prefer to look at patterns and relationships. They often live in the future anticipating what might be. They like possibilities and opportunities to be inventive. They can jump anywhere and (intuitively) leap over steps. They study the overall design to see how parts fit together. Intuitives like change and variety.

Thinking-Feeling are ways of making decisions.
The thinking person decides on the basis of logic and objective considerations. Another way to say it is that they decide with their head. They go by logic and are concerned for truth and justice. They see things as an onlooker from the outside. Thinkers take a long view. They are good at analyzing plans.

The feeling person decides on the basis of personal subjective values or with their hearts. They go by personal conviction and are concerned for relationships and harmony. Feeling types see things as a participant from within a situation. They take an immediate and personal view. They are typically good at understanding people.

Judging-Perceiving are complementary lifestyles.
The judging lifestyle is decisive, planned, and orderly. Judgers like to set clear limits and categories. They feel comfortable establishing

closure. People with the judgment preference handle deadlines and like to plan in advance. Their lifestyle is organized with definite order and structure. Life is best when it is under control.

The perceiving lifestyle is flexible, adaptable, and spontaneous. Perceiving types enjoy being curious and discovering surprises. They like the freedom to explore without limits. They tend to meet deadlines by a last minute rush. They prefer a flexible lifestyle, which means going with the flow. Experiencing life as it happens is their top preference.

Generalization

The following generalizations can be helpful in applying this survey to individual settings:

- People who have the same preferences in the dimensions will seem to *click*, to arrive at decisions more quickly, to be on the same wavelength. Their decisions, however, may suffer because of their preferences, exhibiting blind spots and holes that correspond to the strengths of their less preferred areas.
- People who have different preferences in the dimensions will not see eye to eye on many things and may have difficulty accepting some views, opinions, and actions of the other. The more dimensions in which the two differ, the greater the potential for conflict and misunderstanding of each other. However, decisions resulting from their interaction will benefit from the differing points of view and strengths of each.
- People will normally gravitate toward others who have similar preferences, although people of differing types are often drawn to one another because the strengths of one are admired and needed by the other.
- People's values, beliefs, and actions will be influenced by all four of the stronger dimensions in their typology.
- While a person's preference cannot be changed to its opposite, each person can learn to strengthen the less preferred dimensions.

We are not suggesting that the more traditional organization profiles will be of any less value to the 21st-century association. We are suggesting that in an increasingly diverse workplace there will be an ever-increasing number of individuals with higher levels of need for addressing relationship issues and needs, a more introspective perspective, and stronger desire to feel comfortable about their life condition. This will lead to more balanced valuing of introspection, intuition, feeling, and perceiving as desirable leadership character-istics, as well. In the absence of this balance the 21st century-executive may appear to be manipulative to others.

One way this imbalance is exhibited is by the executive who uses all the current buzzwords like "partnership" or "empowerment," but, in fact, continues to cling to the need to get others to do what he or she wants them to do. Some executives, we are told, have even placed items on a board agenda so that they can be voted down to promote the passage of desired items.

Other executives who have failed to successfully execute the critical 21st-century competencies speak of the importance of good relationships but, when faced with the reality of an employee or volunteer who has difficulty with the relationship or expresses candid needs, becomes defensive and seeks to make the relation-ship issues the other person's problem with language like, "If you weren't so emotional...sensitive...opinionated...this would not be happening."

Other well-intentioned executives may truly seek to hear and understand the opinions of others, but do not have the confidence to maintain consistent behavior among different interest groups. Despite good intentions, the inability to be consistently candid and truthful, or the desire to please everyone eventually earns the executive the label of manipulative.

This aspect of communications is also complex and sensitive. The process of communication—both the message-sending and message-receiving dimensions—is laden with issues of style and value. Essential communication involves thinking, feeling, and acting. Effective execution of the competencies in this area will require executives to use them to govern their own behavior and to model them in their own actions. For some value systems or thinking styles, it is possible that a demand to communicate in a particular way will be perceived as an order to think and act in a particular way. Again, in an increasingly diverse work force, it doesn't matter if this is intent or reality. The behavior of the recipient of such an approach will be based upon a perception of the transaction interpreted through his or her own style and value preferences.

In each of these examples, the energy of the organization becomes diverted to sustaining tension and distrust, reducing the organization's ability to truly achieve excellence. Moving beyond these behaviors requires personal confidence and commitment to self-development—not necessarily cognitive skill development such as business acumen or analytical thinking—but emotional and spiritual maturation and the development of self-understanding. Ultimately, it requires valuing and trusting the self and others.

What Can Happen When Sound Competencies Are Applied?

Several years ago, a very large association faced serious relationship problems. The former executive director, though highly competent in the business of association management, had experienced relationship problems with members and board alike. The board of directors also had difficulty building trust and relationship with the members, and the staff were generally distrustful of both the board and the members.

The primary objective of the new executive director was to rebuild the relationship between the staff and other parts of the organization and to assist the board of directors in rebuilding its new relationships. As a first step, the new director met with key chapter leaders with a three-fold purpose: a) to acknowledge the situation candidly by stating clearly that the bridges between the various parts of the organization were broken and virtually unpassable in their present condition; b) to hear and understand the issues, complaints, and concerns of the chapter leaders and members without judgment or a desire to persuade them of another point of view; and c) to ask them if they were interested in rebuilding the bridges into more healthy organizational relationships.

The next step was to rebuild the staff's enthusiasm for serving the needs of the members. This included a move to a more member-driven decision process, as well as the development of customer service and coaching skills that repositioned the national office from the role of initiator and enforcer to one of co-supporter of the success of each chapter.

As the board worked to develop the direction and shore up some cracks in the infrastructure of the organization, the executive assisted them in developing a leadership strategy that provided for (a) dialogue with dissenting members and (b) the open sharing of information and the rationale behind decisions. Perhaps most important, the leaders helped various stakeholder groups be aware that though they felt, for instance, that advocacy should be eliminated from the association's program of work, other members felt equally as strongly that it must be done. This began to move the disagreement attention away from the board/member direction to a more appropriate member/member direction. The board was then able to facilitate a dialogue among the stakeholders and eventually reach consensus.

One of the executives interviewed observed, "The objective is to create adult/adult rather than adult/child relationships." In this example, the staff and board had been perceived as playing the parental role with chapters and members. By redefining these relationships over time to adult/adult relationships, the energy consumed in unhealthy relationships was rechanneled into achieving the mission of the organization.

CHAPTER 7
Understanding Complex Relationships

Understanding Complex Relationships: A Definition

The ability to understand social, organizational, and technological systems; the ability to evaluate and monitor progress; and the ability to dynamically redesign structures and processes.

For years organizations have been viewed mechanically, by some, with the attendant beliefs that we can tinker with them, oil them, and expect them to run like well-oiled machines. This approach does not acknowledge the complexity, interrelationships, and organic nature of organizations. Nor does it sufficiently recognize the reality that organizations, especially service organizations like associations, are human organizations and as such are unpredictable and idiosyncratic. The effective 21st-century executive is one who understands the complex relationships within the organization.

Key Competencies

- Understands complex organizational relationships and values. Views organization in a holistic, multidimensional manner, focusing attention on root causes, not symptoms. Takes a systemic view, linking cause and effect.
- Uses vision and shared values to inspire others to find where they fit in and can contribute.

- Focuses on root causes.
- Anticipates the unanticipated, and is not paralyzed by change or complexity.
- Emphasizes innovation and creativity; and dynamically recreates models for structure and process.

Multidimensional Thinking

The linear or hierarchical thinking that has served us well in the past is becoming inadequate to meet the challenges of the future. Just as holistic medicine seeks to treat the whole patient, so association management must seek to view service to the membership in a holistic way. It is no longer sufficiently useful to think in terms of labels or segmented thinking, dividing functions into departments such as member services, communications, marketing, and so on. The competent executive understands, for example, that all association activities are in some way member services and that functions like communications or marketing cut across all activity lines.

The more effective approach of the future will be to link all aspects of the organization to the mission and the outcomes, the vision of how the world will be different because of the association's efforts. The association's program of work, structure, and support systems must be in alignment with the vision and direction of the organization.

Since vision and direction are frequently being adjusted based on the changing needs of members in a changing external environment, the successful executive of the 21st century will be more engaged in continuously realigning or redesigning the organization to fit the work that needs to be done to achieve the desired outcomes. This means continually asking questions such as, What is the job that needs to be done here? What is the accountability or outcome expected? What resources are required to make this happen? Who is the best person or group to be accountable for this function?

Using Vision to Inspire Others

It is especially important when matching human resources to the work within the association to provide the opportunity for people to clearly understand and support the vision of what is to be accomplished. The competent association executive of the future will continually use the language of the vision to build this understanding with everyone. He or she will also facilitate self-selection of how each person will participate. Though this will not be possible for every assignment, it is valuable to allow others to decide how they can best contribute to goal achievement.

This approach has the added value of opening the possibility that contributions unforeseen by the executive may come forward. It also ensures that individuals are enthusiastic and committed to the job or task they have, in effect, volunteered to do, and it increases the likelihood that a task and an individual's strengths and interests will be well-matched. In organizations, like associations, that are especially dependent on the effective execution of responsibility by volunteers, such an approach is particularly important.

Using the vision to inspire people's actions and encourage contributions is also critical to being responsive and flexible in an age of change. It is no longer possible for the executive to stop and personally readjust everyone's assignments when change occurs. If each individual clearly understands the desired outcomes of the organization, and the direction, then each individual can take responsibility to make needed adjustments as change occurs. In effect, we make it the responsibility of the individual to stay on course to the desired outcome, rather than uncritically follow previous instructions despite changes in reality.

A critical element in the successful use of vision as a key motivational strategy is that the vision must be owned by many. It cannot be viewed as the vision of the executive or the vision of the board. It must be a vision shared by those who will participate in its pursuit.

Focus on Root Causes

Understanding complex relationships also includes the ability to "see the forest for the trees," i.e. to look for the root cause of a problem, rather than to treat the symptom. A short allegorical story illustrates this important point:

> There once was a small town in the Midwest, fed by a fast-running river through the center of town. Just outside of town the river turned into very treacherous white water rapids.
>
> One day screams came from the river bank. Several of the town's children were floating down the river at great speed heading toward sure death on the rapids. Those nearby immediately began to rescue the children, pulling them from the river.
>
> The calls for help from the rescuers immediately drew all of the townspeople to the task of rescuing the children. As they worked, more and more children floated down river, and the rescuers were barely able to keep up with the challenge. They could not even stop to rest as the children came one after the other.
>
> Eventually, one of the townspeople began to walk up river, away from the task at hand. The others were furious, screaming things like, "Coward, how can you walk away from our children?," until the would-be deserter, continuing up river, was heard to say, "I think it is time for someone to go see who is throwing our children into the river!"

Responding to an obvious crisis is the job of many. Remembering to walk upriver and find the root cause of the problem is the task of contemporary leadership. When membership begins to decline, it may be useful to increase recruitment efforts, but it is also essential to find out the root cause of the decline. When member complaints appear, it is important to address the immediate issue, but it is also essential to evaluate the process being used to meet member needs. And when conflicts appear between individuals or groups of people, it is also essential to look behind the stated reasons to the fundamental truth that has created the problem. It is only by accurately diagnosing the root cause that we can remove the unwanted problem from our organization.

Responding to the Unanticipated

We discussed earlier the changing nature of change and its increasing unpredictability. Understanding complex relationships is critical to an executive's ability to be responsive and flexible in the face of unanticipated changes. There are two discoverable insights of particular importance here. First, when unanticipated change occurs we must ask, "How does this affect everything else we are doing?" To respond to the change without a reasonable answer to this question will do little more than treat a symptom. Second, change must be viewed opportunistically or it will paralyze the executive and ultimately the organization.

A competent executive of the 21st century will skillfully call together the people necessary to look at the impact of change upon the organization and seek the opportunities imbedded within it. The executive will embrace the possibilities rather than apply a surface response to the situation. Above all, he or she will enlist the viewpoint of others in identifying the appropriate response. In a world characterized by rapidly developing and changing volumes of information—the complexity of alternatives and options will multiply—and specialization of expertise and perspectives will grow accordingly. The 21st-century executive will appreciate the new reality that it is less likely that in such a world any one person or small group of like people will know enough about all things of significance to make a good decision alone.

Dynamic Innovation and Creativity

The successful executive of tomorrow understands the critical importance of continually re-engineering structures and processes to meet emerging realities. This can best be done by continually focusing on the outcomes to be achieved, and then evaluating the strategic forces both hindering and supporting achievement of the goals. Therefore, it will be important to create a culture within the organization that recognizes the importance of *no sacred cows*. If an organization or an executive operates with the handicap that only some important things can be redesigned but others cannot, true innovation and creativity will not likely become a reality within the organization.

Many of the executives interviewed spoke of moving toward more of an "ad hocracy" approach to structure. Project teams were also frequently mentioned. In such approaches, the formalized structure of the organization is limited or kept to a minimum. Project teams or ad hoc work groups are created to address issues or focus areas. These groups are redesigned or eliminated as the needs change or an issue is successfully resolved. This approach is especially useful in diminishing the natural inclination toward creating or preserving sacred cows because it creates the expectation that all things will be reformed as the need arises.

This approach will also be especially useful in helping an organization move from evaluating or judging people to evaluating and adjusting the processes people use. Considerable research suggests that when problems occur within an organization, it is rarely a problem with individuals, but more likely a problem with the institutionalized processes being used by individuals to accomplish their work.

As we discussed these competencies with executives identified as having demonstrated those competencies, they shared several observations with us. Among them:

> It is so important to focus on the forest not the trees. Otherwise, each crisis that comes along is the most important. And suddenly we find that no one has asked the question, "Is this important in the first place?"

I try to always remember not to focus on whose fault it is or the employee involved. Instead, I try to determine the systemic or process problem that created the situation."

CHAPTER 8
Acquiring and Using Information

Acquiring and Using Information: A Definition

The ability to acquire and evaluate, organize and interpret information, and communicate it in a way that is understood and relevant.

Information is power—a familiar bromide with a long history. This idea led to many executives guarding information in order to attain and hold power. In today's technologically assisted information age, however, knowledge becomes the real currency of power—what we do with the information and how we apply it. There is simply too much information for any one person to hold enough of it.

Key Competencies

- Asks the right questions of the right sources, using good counsel, and investing in the collection of good information.
- Balances quantitative information with qualitative and intuitive information; balances own experience and instincts with the opinion of experts.
- Trusts ability to acquire information; does not need to hold information.
- Views information as a window to new opportunity.

- Shares information freely.
- Communicates by full disclosure of information.

Asking the Right Questions

Asking the right questions is a pivotal competency of the effective 21st-century executive—whether seeking good counsel, information from members about needs and wants, or information from volunteers or employees to support accomplishment of their work. Questions can be used both to lead others to a point of view or used to build an information rich environment in which to make decisions. In this chapter we are exploring the latter.

Seeking good counsel requires a comfort with admitting as an executive that we do not know everything about a subject. This has generally been easier in subject arenas such as legal requirements, finance, data processing, or other such specialty areas. However, in today's complex and information rich business environment, it is also important to be willing to seek the counsel of others who are in a position to add to our perspective. Into the 21st century, this will increasingly mean seeking counsel from others who have a differing point of view, or from those who process information in a different way or style than we do. The willingness to operate from a perspective of "not knowing all" will be more valuable to the executive of tomorrow than operating from the more traditional model of "I know it all."

Increasingly, in the creation of meaningful information from members, questions that merely establish whether something is good or bad are becoming archaic, perhaps with the exception of customer service surveys specifically designed to identify quantifiable satisfaction levels. With increasing frequency, the most useful questions to seek information on which to make defensible decisions about the future are questions that provide qualitative information of substance. Examples of such questions include, What are the most critical issues you face in your profession today? What frustrates you most about your professional reality? What do you anticipate your profession will look like five years from now? What is the one need you have that is not being filled now, but if it were being filled, would make a significant contribution to your professional success? It is answers to these kinds of questions that will give the knowledge-based associations meaningful data on which to plan for the future.

When seeking to support volunteers or employees, it is often tempting to give answers before having enough information, or to ask questions that are results oriented such as, When will this project be finished? Or what have you accomplished? However, it is more likely questions such as, What are you trying to accomplish? What difficulties are you experiencing? and What don't you have now that if you had access to it would allow you to accomplish this task more quickly or better? will provide executives committed to supporting the work of others with the information they will need to successfully implement their intentions.

Balancing Types of Information

These types of questions lead the executive to a rich pool of qualitative information that, in service environments like associations, can be far more useful than shallow quantitative data on membership trends or isolated statistical surveys. Perhaps historical overreliance on quantitative data stems from the influence of manufacturing industries during the industrial age, or perhaps from the absoluteness of numbers and the more comfortable feeling that with quantitative data we can be sure. Whatever the reason, it will be important for 21st-century executives to balance quantitative data with at least equal parts, and probably more parts, of qualitative information.

One way this commitment to data gathering will miss its mark is when an executive crafts questions designed to support a personal vision or belief, rather than to collect information that may suggest a shift in direction is needed. The competent executive will be one who is open to finding out the truth about how others view things, not one who seeks to validate personal beliefs.

It is also as critical for the competent executive to rely on his or her own experience and intuition—the instinct of what will work or what is coming in the future. In the words of one executive, "Intuition is based partly on experience and we need to learn to trust what we have learned. This is really necessary in the complex and rapidly changing environment we now work in."

That rapidly changing and complex work environment demands timely decisions made in an information-rich environment. It will be necessary to widely expand the common definition of information-rich to include intuition and qualitative data, for association executives and the groups they lead to reach peak performance. As several interviewees pointed out, it is "very important to test and validate assumptions so that adjustments can be made to the original decision."

Trusting Versus Holding

As we mentioned in the beginning of this chapter, there is simply too much information available today for any executive to try to personally hold all of the information he or she needs. There is a growing perspective that trying to retain too much information in memory may, in fact, reduce an individual's capacity to notice, receive, and process new information. Based on this perspective, tomorrow's executive can and should begin to focus attention on having access to good sources of information flow, rather than attempting to cram more and more data into his or her own personal memory bank.

A Window to New Opportunity

Information can be viewed as a window to new opportunities and a way to continually build new ways of looking at the association. Seizing this opportunity, however, is dependent on the executive's ability to view information neutrally and with curiosity—not judging information as good or bad. In the words of one executive,

In order to fully benefit from the value of new information, we must be willing to risk endangering our existing paradigms. It is only through a willingness to change our beliefs and perspectives that we can truly build new ways of looking at our organizations.

Sharing Freely

It is widely agreed that knowledge, not just information, will be the competitive advantage of the 21st century. This means that the success will be achieved by executives who are able to assist their association in turning information into knowledge for members, volunteer leaders, and staff.

Sharing information freely is critical to this process. It is by conversing about the information that people build and reshape it into knowledge directly learned and experienced by many. It is through direct experience, consideration, and application that information becomes knowledge. And, it is knowledge that is required for individuals to respond actively and effectively to the shifting landscape of their environment—whether within the association as an enterprise or within the still larger context of the members' world.

Examination of the case studies and the interviews with effective executives of the competencies, both identified the withholding of information as a tactic of the ineffective executive. These ineffective executives were characterized as insecure executives who seek to have power over rather than power with the members or staff. In one of the case studies examined, a consultant from our firm had the experience of facilitating a planning session with one such executive. That experience is illustrative of ineffective execution of these competencies. At each turn in the conversation, this executive would inject a new piece of information in "guru-like" fashion. This information had not been shared with the planning participants in advance, so that it could enrich the decision process. Instead it was used to create dependence on the executive. It was also being used to see how the wind was blowing—to find out what others were thinking—then to move them off a point not supported by the executive by adding information that was not supportive of the point.

Over several years of this approach, the executive had, in fact, created the position of "guru" and his board would continually turn to him for the final pronouncement on any decision. For this association, this limited the organization's vision and capability to that of one person, rather than ultimately combining the collective vision and capabilities of the leadership group into a greater whole. This is one example of withholding information as a tactic of control and manipulation—an ineffective execution of competencies related to acquiring and using information.

Information can also be used for control by sharing certain kinds of information with different groups, thereby fragmenting group unity—dividing and conquering. Once again, the executive who chooses this technique may enjoy a temporary feeling of security, but he or she is also ensuring that the association will operate at greatly reduced levels of potential and performance.

Communication

The executive that is highly competent in acquiring and using information requires an additional ability for truly effective execution of competence in this area. He or she must be able to communicate by full disclosure the rationale behind any decision. It may not matter how sound a decision is, if there is no ability to build understanding and acceptance of it among the appropriate stakeholders within the organization. It is through effective communication of information and decision rationale that leaders are able to create knowledge within the organization. It will be knowledge that transforms the culture and behavior to what will be necessary in the future.

One simple but insightful example of these competencies working well was provided by an interviewee:

I sensed that something was missing from the format of a particular annual meeting. It was nothing I could put my finger on, but I sensed it could be improved. I spoke with several of the members of the meeting group to get a sense of their needs and feelings about the current set up. I then consulted with an expert who is developing new approaches to meetings. He described a radically new concept that would be quite a departure from our normal way of doing things. I then went back to the group and built their acceptance to try it out—though a radical departure, my intuition told me it might serve us well. We tried it and it was a resounding success.

CHAPTER 9
Valuing and Using Technology

Valuing and Using Technology: A Definition

The ability to integrate information, knowledge, capacity, technological tools, and processes to effectively achieve the desired purposes.

C losely related to information competencies is valuing and using technology. This may, in fact, be one place where the interdependence of the competencies is very obvious.

We cannot be effective in this area unless we are able to articulate what success will look like; determine what we need; trust the advice and counsel of experts; make balanced decisions based on quantitative, qualitative, and intuitive information; and demonstrate a willingness to risk success.

As we identified in Chapter 4, effective associations are exceptional candidates for significant use of technology because they are information/knowledge-driven organizations. Yet, as we also discussed, support for the necessary human and material investments in technology does not always meet the demand or opportunity within organizations.

This is further exacerbated by the reality that it may be in the area of technology that we are experiencing the most rapid change. Additionally, many 20th-century executives are not technologically confident. In the words of one executive, "I am a Luddite at heart! But the association relies on technology. I have been required to see the importance of this."

Key Competencies

- Articulates future direction and needs in order to acquire the tools needed for success.
- Confidently and willingly ventures into the unknown, relying on the advice of technological experts, in order to provide the tools required to get the job done effectively.
- Provides others with the tools required and the support to be confident and proficient in their use.

The Articulation of Needs

"Though we must rely on the technological experts to bring our attention to the systems we need, the really tough part is having the discipline and the patience to articulate what we need this system to do," says one executive who demonstrates successful execution of these competencies. As with many of the competencies identified in this study, the ability to articulate the vision and future direction of the organization is essential to effectively executing key competencies related to technology. This includes what we are trying to accomplish for members, what we are trying to create in the way of information bases and communications linkages, what we are trying to process, and what we are trying to create in terms of work tools. Some associations are even beginning to recognize and install a powerful link between consensus building and the use of technology.

Effective oversight of technological decisions does not begin at the bottom, i.e., with the specific request for a piece of information. It begins with the articulation of what is desired as an outcome. The solution or application is then built on the intention, not in response to a specific request. Effective execution of this competency ensures that the necessary links occur between the association's strategic plan, business lines and specific programs, and the current or proposed systems needed to support the achievement of intended outcomes.

The assessment of systems needs includes three primary areas of consideration:

Functionality: the identification of additional functions or systems processing that must be developed;

Data Content: the identification of new or changing data elements that must be collected and managed in order to support knowledge building and decision-making processes; and

Data Access and Retrieval: who needs to access data, when does that access need to occur, and what type of access needs to be available?

The 21st-century executive will be frequently engaged in considering the future direction of the organization as the foundation for examining and creating technological systems. Additionally, the 21st-century executive will learn to consider the human dimensions of technology use—that is, the nontechnological processes in the association used to accomplish the work—while designing technology and initiatives. Failure to consider both aspects can result in (a) reliance on how things have worked in the past as an indicator of what will work in the future, (b) installation of new systems not used to purchased capacity or (c) disastrous, attendant consequences for other important elements of the organization's culture or operations. In the area of technology, decision making is especially dangerous because increasingly rapid technological advances will make old ways of doing things archaic and costly in increasingly short time frames.

For the 21st-century executive who wants to promote association decision making based on shared, relevant, and reliable knowledge—continual attention to such complex issues in a continuously

evolving environment will assume increasing importance—
and consume an increasing proportion of executive time.

Venturing Into the Unknown

Venturing into the unknown of technological systems is critical for
an association to stay on the front edge of its curve; it is a critical
area to risking success. But it is also an area of significant financial
risk. This double-edged sword challenges the executive of the
future to apply finely honed discernment skills, especially in the
area of people selection. The ability to select knowledgeable, trust-
worthy guides with whom one can communicate effectively
is a pivotal necessity.

The Himalayan Mountains often attract expert climbers who are
essentially unfamiliar with the terrain they are about to challenge.
The successful climbers have learned to rely upon native guides
called "sherpas" who grew up navigating the mountains and climb
constantly to maintain familiarity with a constantly shifting landscape. Over the years the most recognized climbers have developed
true partnerships with their sherpa—with each successive climb
bringing both increased challenge and reward.

Because of the special importance of this discernment and
selection process and the dynamically changing nature of technological development, more and more executives will find it strategically essential to establish long-term relationships with the right
"sherpas." They will recognize systems design and refinement as an
ongoing process that will require coherent support. They will not
view the technology needed to support a knowledge based association as an isolated project or a series of piecemeal operations.

When discussing this competency with effective executors
of competencies in this area, one executive offered a simple,
but useful approach:

> We invest heavily in determining the needs of the organiza-
> tion, beginning with the outcomes we desire. We then work

with proven experts to discern the alternative approaches available to us and the risks and rewards of each. Perhaps most important, we test and evaluate these alternatives, including seeking the experience of other organizations who have used these approaches. We then use this feedback to make regret-free decisions.

The absence of these competencies or avoidance of issues related to them because of fear of making a mistake—or undervaluing what one does not know and understand—leads to a "knee-jerk reactor syndrome." This is a situation encountered throughout our examination of case studies where ineffective execution of competencies related to technology was observed. Decisions or attention are delayed too long. When attention is finally forced upon the executive, he or she only attends to the squeaking wheel and does not look at systems holistically. The result is too little too late; a system held together by a hope, and a song and tap dance before the funders—rather than a well-integrated, functional, and cost-effective working system. The full financial loss potentially incurred by such an approach can go unidentified for years. Our case studies suggest it is usually far greater than any financial risk that would have been incurred by a proactive decision made earlier in time.

Providing What Others Need

Fear, often when combined with a culture of Scrooge-like tendencies, can lead to an environment of stinginess in the workplace. In other words, people are asked to perform their jobs without benefit of the tools they need to be most effective. Effective 21st-century executives will provide others with the tools they need to get the job done effectively.

This competency extends well beyond providing the equipment or system required. It also includes providing the training, support, and encouragement needed to make maximum use of the technological tools available. It is not enough to provide a system or even the training. Ongoing support is required, as well. The most effective use of evolving technology will, for some time, require the availability of an up-to-date coach, someone to help subject area specialists employing a new tool. As one technology competent executive observed,

> Following a major systems installation, we did a thorough evaluation of what was happening. We learned that the employ-ees needed a "helpmate," rather than more training. They needed someone available for hands-on assistance with how to use the system better as they encountered potential new applications. Training is important, but we found that by providing a helpmate we significantly increased confidence and performance.

Who Drives Innovation?

It will certainly be important for the effective 21st-century executive to develop and use technology-related competencies for the benefit of the organization. In our conversations with technologically effec-tive executives, it also became apparent that an intellectual attribute shared by many of them was a recognition of the importance of letting go of hierarchical decision making and allowing the users to drive the creation and innovation of the systems. As in many of the competency areas we have explored, the 21st-century executive will increasingly be dedicated to seeing that the people who can best have input and make decisions are given the opportunity to do so.

The 21st-century executive will interactively guide the com-puter, communications, work process and human interaction of a knowledge-based association. In fact, the systematic approaches for accomplishing this guided interaction in an association are them-selves a technology in the broader sense of the word. When such technologies are in place, successful executives of the future will take more pride in seeing that a good decision is made than they will take in personally having made a good decision.

CHAPTER 10
Deployment of Resources

Deployment of Resources: A Definition

The ability to set priorities and allocate time, money, materials, space, volunteer, and staff resources.

I t is no secret that there are far more ways to meet member needs than there are association resources. This is a long-held truth of association management. In Chapter 2 we explored the idea that focusing on serving the common self-interests of the members, even when that requires doing fewer things of higher value for more targeted groups, will make the most effective use of our resources. In this chapter we will expand this notion to explore the increasing importance strategic planning and organizational alignment will play in the effective deployment of resources.

Key Competencies

- Values strategic planning and links all organizational systems, structures and decisions to this plan.
- Focuses on long-term strategic outcomes, the right thing to do, not simply how to do things right.
- Empowers others by providing the authority and resources required by individual accountabilities.

- Prioritizes based on impact, immediacy, and consequence when making strategic decisions about resources.
- Uses the intangible assets of the organization to create results and opportunity.

Effective Deployment of Resources Begins With Strategic Planning

Strategic planning is the process of a) developing a vision of a desirable future; b) determining the common interests of the members and the realities of the environment in which the membership and their association operates; c) establishing the mission, goals, and strategies of the organization based on this information; d) identifying the program of work needed to achieve the mission and goals; e) aligning the organization's structures and systems to match the kind of work called for in the plan; and f) continually evaluating and adjusting the plan and its supporting elements based on changes in the environment, new information, or experience in implementation. The effective deployment of resources in a 21st-century organization will be done in alignment with the elements of a responsive but flexible strategic plan, driven by a continually maintained consensus on what will constitute success.

Doing the Right Things

Resource allocation can best be done when the organization assesses both issues of effectiveness and issues of efficiency. In other words, the organization must determine the right things to do, before it can rationally determine how to deploy resources to do things right. We are all familiar with organizations that are doing things right, but are doing all the wrong things. Until the association achieves the necessary degree of agreement on what it is trying to accomplish, there may be little chance that it will be able to organize and deploy its resources in a way that produces the efficiencies required for peak performance or quality service.

In the absence of an outcome-oriented strategic plan, every good idea that comes along, or is heard by leadership at a recent meeting, is an equal candidate for implementation. Sometimes this leads to several key working units moving in different or counter-productive directions.

Organizing for Alignment

Consider the following diagram. Think of your organization as three inter-related arenas. The arena of mission is related to direction. The arena of operations involves how you organize systems, people, and responsibilities in a way that effectively deploys resources. The arena of group process includes the behaviors exhibited by individuals as they seek to achieve outcomes by using the systems we have established. In reality, the interactive elements of an organization like an association are much more complex than this figure reflects. (See Appendix B for elements of the organization and a snapshot self-appraisal instrument to assess organizational health.)

Exhibit 12: Three Arenas of Associations as Organizations

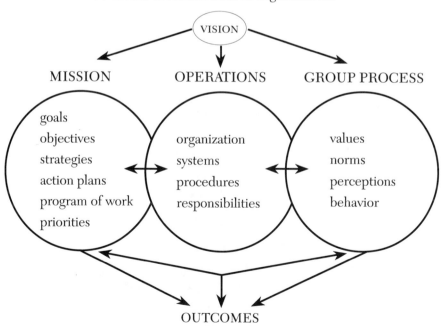

Even in this simplified diagram, however, as interrelated arenas, whenever a change or shift occurs in one arena, it throws the others out of alignment—they require adjustment. This diagram emphasizes the critical importance of matching all resource deployment decisions to both the direction established by the strategic plan and to the culture of the organization.

Let's try to illustrate this with a simple, but powerful, example. Several years ago there was a major airline that made a commitment to quality customer service. It held employee rallies, it hung banners, and made all kinds of noise about quality. It had done some market research and determined that one of the most important things to its customers was baggage being handled without damage and getting to the same place as the passenger on time. So they ordered the baggage handlers to pay attention to quality. They told them how important it was; they empowered them to do it. However, they had a formal system called their "compensation structure," a key element of human resource deployment. This system paid baggage handlers a base salary determined by time and longevity, and a group bonus based on the number of units of baggage handled in an hour. Now, be a baggage handler for a moment. If you have a choice between "quality" performance, and putting needed dollars in your pocket, which are you going to choose? Until the compensation structure was realigned to better fit the behavior the organization was trying to encourage, it was unlikely that, no matter how intelligent or well-articulated the goal, it would be achieved.

In a world characterized by increasingly rapid and dramatic change, it will be increasingly critical to continually evaluate organizational alignment. To what extent does the organization:

- Possess the knowledge and skills, the competencies, necessary for peak performance?
- Possess the information necessary?
- Provide intrinsic rewards that give people a sense of accomplishment, independence, and social status?

- Have the appropriate physical and organization structure in place?
- Organize for effective decision making?
- Create critical relationships between the working parts of the organization?
- Provide tools required to get the job done?
- Match reward systems and personnel practices to the desired outcomes?
- Have an informal structure—the real policy manual of norms, values, and behaviors, that support the desired outcomes?
- Invest heavily in the goal areas articulated as important in the strategic plan?

The effective executive of the 21st century will find an increasingly greater proportion of time and intellectual capital expended in considering alignment issues. The ability to maintain an effective fit through resource decisions tied to outcomes articulated in a strategic planning process will be increasingly critical to organizational success in an environment characterized by diverse demands and limited resources. It will require an executive who understands how to ensure not only that things are done right, but that the organization is doing the right things.

Empowering Others

The extent to which there is a match between authority, responsibility, and capacity for any task being undertaken by an individual or organizational unit will be critical to issues of organizational alignment and resource deployment. *Authority* refers to the extent to which the organizational unit is able to commit the association. *Responsibility* refers to what the organization is dependent on the individual or unit to do. *Capacity* refers to the extent to which the individual or unit possesses the resources required (information, expertise, time, and tools) to accomplish the responsibility. Twentieth-century associations are notorious for assigning responsibility, sometimes even with adequate resources, but without the necessary authority to carry out the task. The executive of the 21st century will have to successfully and routinely negotiate and balance all three of these components of accountability.

One executive interviewed to validate the hypothesis developed from the case studies described an almost zero-based staff accountability system implemented to align authority, responsibilities, and capacity with the demands of a strategic plan:

> Following the completion of our strategic plan, we embarked on a major realignment of job responsibilities. As a group, we identified the accountabilities imbedded in the plan and carefully described what success would look like as these accountabilities are carried out. This evaluation was done without consideration of who are the people available to take on the accountabilities.
>
> We then identified the resources required for each accountability, including time. For instance, some accountabilities required 50% time or one-half a full-time equivalent. Others required 200% or two full-time equivalents. This approach allowed us to more accurately determine our human resource needs.
>
> Existing employees were then given the opportunity to apply for each of the jobs emerging from the accountabilities. This required courage and cooperation on the part of the employee group, but the rewards were significant. We ended up with individuals well-matched to the work, organized in a fashion linked to the strategic plan, with definable outcomes on which to evaluate organizational performance.
>
> There were also several secondary benefits. Because accountabilities are now clearly defined, there is little duplica-

tion of effort among employee groups and no time wasted asking for unnecessary approvals or permission. We are able to focus our attention on evaluation and adjustment for quality performance.

Program Priorities

We began this section with the observation that typically there are more opportunities to respond to member needs, wants, and expectations than there are resources to meet them. Increasingly, resource deployment in the 21st century will also need to operate on two basic assumptions: a) Focus is important—i.e., it is better to provide fewer high quality programs in response to a set of focused, common interests, than to provide mediocre or low quality programs or services in many areas; and b) given the need for resources, organizations generally will not directly duplicate the services of other organizations, especially if the same pocket is funding all these organizations.

We offer two approaches to prioritizing used by highly effective association executives. The first applies to prioritizing programs and services. Assessment of program priorities may be carried out by evaluating three critical areas:

- **Program Attractiveness:** the degree to which the program or service is attractive to the organization as a basis for current and future resource deployment. Factors to be measured in this evaluation include (a) the extent to which the program is congruent with the mission of the organization, (b) attractiveness to members, (c) the degree to which the competencies and resources required can also support other program areas, and (d) the extent of resources required.

- **Competitive Position:** the degree to which the organization is in a strong position to support the program or service. This component measures (a) customer loyalty, (b) size of the market, (c) track record, (d) the ability to produce a better quality than competitors, and (e) the availability of the necessary skills to support the program.

- **Alternative Coverage:** the extent to which other organizations can, or may be positioned to, serve the same clients through similar programs or services. In other words, is someone else responding to the same member need with a different or similar product.

In its simplest form, this assessment can identify those programs to aggressively grow (high program attractiveness, strong competitive position) or aggressively divest (high program attractiveness, but weak competitive position).

Strategic Priorities

It will also be increasingly important for resource deployment decisions to ascertain which strategies will be most important to the success of the organization. In a simple but powerful form, this may be done by asking two basic questions: (a) What are the factors that exist, or could be created, that will support our movement toward desired outcomes? (b) What are the factors that block our movement toward these outcomes?

When these factors have been identified they may be evaluated and prioritized based on three criteria emerging as strategic variables in selectively deploying resources in a 21st-century association.

- **Impact:** A measure of breadth of importance. How basic is the factor? How many other things depend on it or are related to it? This is a measure of strategic importance related to relationships.

- **Consequence:** A measure of depth of importance. How bad or good will it be if it happens? This is a measure of strategic importance related to intensity.

- **Immediacy:** A measure of the importance of the opportunity and sequence. How much time is available? Is there a chronological order? This is a measure of strategic importance related to time.

The competent executive of the 21st century will use relevant criteria and rational approaches to make defensible decisions about resource allocation. For resource deployment decisions to be perceived as sound, strategic decisions that maximize use of the organization's available resources, key stakeholders will more and more see that an objective logic was employed to make those decisions. Approaches, like those described here, will be increasingly important to executives who will need to be able to demonstrate the logic behind sometimes controversial or politically painful decisions.

Using Intangible Assets

History, reputation, organization credibility and momentum created by success—these are not assets found on any association balance sheet. They are, however, powerful resources used by the most successful association executives. Viewing the organization holistically and opportunistically often means seeing into the unseen, deploying the forces of reputation or enthusiasm generated by momentum to a task, just as we deploy tangible resources. Perhaps it is in this way, the executive of the 21st century will most resemble a successful coach, orchestra conductor, or magician.

Epilogue

As we have said throughout this book, because associations are people intensive, human capital is the greatest resource of the industry. It is also true that human beings are often unpredictable. There is, therefore, no way to delineate in absolute terms a prescription for executive success in any given organization. In other words, these competencies do not come with an unconditional money back guarantee.

We have examined many areas in this work that are situational, others that may even seem paradoxical. Each executive or association leader will need to find a balance, the appropriate balance for his or her organization, and this balance will change as the association and its environment change.

We also assume that executives as individuals will each exhibit certain areas of strength among these competencies and certain areas of less comfort. We are not suggesting that every executive must demonstrate equal competence in every area. We are suggesting that awareness of the shifting paradigms within the association industry, and awareness of their attendant impact on the requirements of executives will go a long way toward ensuring success for the committed executive in the 21st century.

We wish each reader success in seeking to find the appropriate balance of competencies for you and your organization. We encourage you to be willing to create new paradigms for your own behaviors, and to be willing to risk success on behalf of yourself and your organization. There is no doubt that the future will be different than the past, and there is no reason to anticipate that the future will be any less bright than the past we have known.

SECTION III

Self-Appraisal Tools

APPENDIX A
About the Perceptual
Self-Assessment

The following self-study was created as a tool for individuals to develop a personal portrait of knowledge and competence about the 21st-century competencies.

The instrument is self-explanatory. Rate yourself on two scales relevant to each competency:

- The degree of knowledge you perceive you possess about a competency; and
- the degree of confidence you perceive you feel in terms of your current ability to successfully execute a competency.

Each cluster of competencies is followed by a synopsis sheet to assess your relative strengths, opportunities/needs, and vulnerabilities in each cluster of skills.

The survey ends with a summary sheet that allows you to create a personal profile based on your self-perceptions.

The primary uses of the Perceptual Self-Assessment are to (a) enable you to set forth an appropriate plan for professional self-development and (b) determine what special talents you bring to any team in which you lead or participate.

Perceptual Self-Assessment
Critical Competencies For Association Executives

Cluster A: Interpersonal Skills

Definition: Ability to work as a member of a group, teach others, serve members, lead, negotiate, and work well with people from culturally diverse backgrounds.

Degree of Knowledge
(Formal Study: exposure through books and/or courses; Experiential learning: have successfully employed this behavior on more than one occasion.)

Degree of Confidence

In-Depth Knowledge	Some Knowledge	Little or No Knowledge	COMPETENCIES	Do Very Well	Get By Most of Time	Expect To Have Problems
|-------|-------|-------|-------|-------|			A1. Respects and values differences of personal style, opinion and culture, and facilitates resolution of differences between others.	|-------|-------|-------|-------|-------|		
|-------|-------|-------|-------|-------|			A2. Skillfully builds consensus among diverse groups.	|-------|-------|-------|-------|-------|		
|-------|-------|-------|-------|-------|			A3. Able to hear and *understand* others.	|-------|-------|-------|-------|-------|		
|-------|-------|-------|-------|-------|			A4. Clearly communicates true feelings and thoughts with compassion and forthrightness, and is able to directly ask for what is needed.	|-------|-------|-------|-------|-------|		
|-------|-------|-------|-------|-------|			A5. Oriented toward "can-do" approach in meeting the needs of others.	|-------|-------|-------|-------|-------|		
|-------|-------|-------|-------|-------|			A6. Looks for ways to support and enhance others' strengths.	|-------|-------|-------|-------|-------|		
|-------|-------|-------|-------|-------|			A7. Able to observe, question and discern issues and choices without judgment.	|-------|-------|-------|-------|-------|		
|-------|-------|-------|-------|-------|			A8. Open, receptive and willing to risk failure.	|-------|-------|-------|-------|-------|		
|-------|-------|-------|-------|-------|			A9. Congruent in words and actions.	|-------|-------|-------|-------|-------|		

Downside: Rigid, defensive, manipulating, controlling and fearful. Unwilling to take personal risks. Often results in indirect communication, fragmentation of groups and a misunderstanding of the needs and intent of others.

AREA SYNOPSIS

Place the number of each competency on the appropriate scale below.

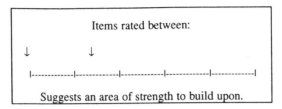

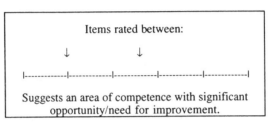

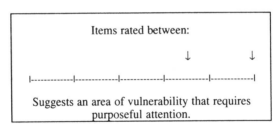

Cluster B: Valuing and Using Technology

Definition: Ability to integrate information, knowledge, capacities, technological tools, and processes to effectively achieve desired purposes.

Degree of Knowledge
*(Formal Study: exposure through books
and/or courses; Experiential learning:
have successfully employed this
behavior on more than one occasion.)*

Degree of Confidence

In-Depth Knowledge	Some Knowledge	Little or No Knowledge	COMPETENCIES	Do Very Well	Get By Most of Time	Expect To Have Problems
|------|------|------|------|------|			B1. Confident and willing to venture into the unknown, relying on the input of technological experts and seeking continual innovation that will provide others with the tools to get the job done effectively.	|------|------|------|------|------|		
|------|------|------|------|------|			B2. Able to articulate future direction and needs in order to acquire the tools needed for success.	|------|------|------|------|------|		
|------|------|------|------|------|			B3. Able to build the confidence and acceptance of others who may be fearful and resistant.	|------|------|------|------|------|		
|------|------|------|------|------|			B4. Understands the importance of continual investment in innovation and user training.	|------|------|------|------|------|		
|------|------|------|------|------|			B5. Views technology as a tool, not an obstacle or tyrant.	|------|------|------|------|------|		

Downside: Knee-jerk reactor—too little, too late. Paralyzed by fear and ego—fears or undervalues what they do not understand. Uses past as an indicator of the future. Invests in equipment, but not in user training and upgrade. Stingy—does not view job as giving people the tools they need.

AREA SYNOPSIS

Place the number of each competency on the appropriate scale below.

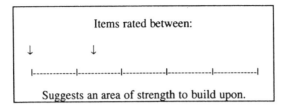

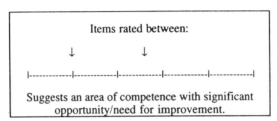

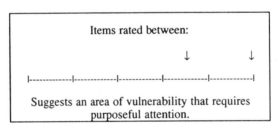

Cluster C: Acquiring and Using Information

Definition: Ability to acquire and evaluate information, organize and interpret that information, and communicate it in a way that is understood and relevant.

Degree of Knowledge
*(Formal Study: exposure through books
and/or courses; Experiential learning:
have successfully employed this
behavior on more than one occasion.)*

Degree of Confidence

In-Depth Knowledge	Some Knowledge	Little or No Knowledge	COMPETENCIES	Do Very Well	Get By Most of Time	Expect To Have Problems
├─────┼─────┼─────┼─────┼─────┤			C1. Ability to ask the right questions of the right sources of information; able to use good counsel.	├─────┼─────┼─────┼─────┼─────┤		
├─────┼─────┼─────┼─────┼─────┤			C2. Continually seeks a balance of new quantitative, qualitative, and intuitive information and is willing to invest in the collection of this information.	├─────┼─────┼─────┼─────┼─────┤		
├─────┼─────┼─────┼─────┼─────┤			C3. Relies on own experience and intuition to evaluate the data—does not rely solely on "expert" opinion.	├─────┼─────┼─────┼─────┼─────┤		
├─────┼─────┼─────┼─────┼─────┤			C4. Understands that information is power and shares it freely.	├─────┼─────┼─────┼─────┼─────┤		
├─────┼─────┼─────┼─────┼─────┤			C5. Integrates the use of qualitative, quantitative, and intuitive information to allow for timely decision making.	├─────┼─────┼─────┼─────┼─────┤		
├─────┼─────┼─────┼─────┼─────┤			C6. Communicates information by full disclosure focusing on outcomes and building understanding, thereby continually transforming knowledge, culture, and behavior.	├─────┼─────┼─────┼─────┼─────┤		
├─────┼─────┼─────┼─────┼─────┤			C7. Trusts ability to acquire information, does not need to "hold" information.	├─────┼─────┼─────┼─────┼─────┤		
├─────┼─────┼─────┼─────┼─────┤			C8. Views information as a window to new opportunity; continually builds new ways of looking at things based on new information; does not judge information as good or bad.	├─────┼─────┼─────┼─────┼─────┤		

Downside: Pursues own vision and opinion regardless of data or member needs, or only seeks information that will support own vision and opinion. Withholds information as a tactic of control. Able to make good decisions, but unable to use information to communicate rationale.

AREA SYNOPSIS

Place the number of each competency on the appropriate scale below.

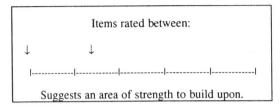

Items rated between:

↓   ↓

|------------|------------|------------|------------|------------|

Suggests an area of strength to build upon.

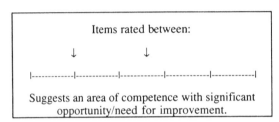

Items rated between:

↓   ↓

|------------|------------|------------|------------|------------|

Suggests an area of competence with significant
opportunity/need for improvement.

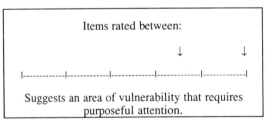

Items rated between:

↓   ↓

|------------|------------|------------|------------|------------|

Suggests an area of vulnerability that requires
purposeful attention.

Cluster D: Understanding Complex Relationships

Definition: Ability to understand social, organizational, and technological systems; ability to evaluate and monitor progress; ability to design new structures and processes.

Degree of Knowledge
(Formal Study: exposure through books and/or courses; Experiential learning: have successfully employed this behavior on more than one occasion.)

Degree of Confidence

In-Depth Knowledge	Some Knowledge	Little or No Knowledge	COMPETENCIES	Do Very Well	Get By Most of Time	Expect To Have Problems
|-----|-----|-----|-----|-----|				D1. Understands complex organizational relationships and values. Views organization in a holistic, multidimensional manner.	|-----|-----|-----|-----|-----|		
|-----|-----|-----|-----|-----|				D2. Focuses attention on root causes, not symptoms.	|-----|-----|-----|-----|-----|		
|-----|-----|-----|-----|-----|				D3. Uses vision and shared values to inspire others to find where they fit in and can contribute.	|-----|-----|-----|-----|-----|		
|-----|-----|-----|-----|-----|				D4. Anticipates the unanticipated, and is not paralyzed by complexity.	|-----|-----|-----|-----|-----|		
|-----|-----|-----|-----|-----|				D5. Emphasizes innovation and creativity; not focused on correction of weaknesses.	|-----|-----|-----|-----|-----|		
|-----|-----|-----|-----|-----|				D6. Understands how to guide rather than force change by driving out definition of what success will look like at the highest level of common interest.	|-----|-----|-----|-----|-----|		
|-----|-----|-----|-----|-----|				D7. Willing to create new models for structure and process.	|-----|-----|-----|-----|-----|		
|-----|-----|-----|-----|-----|				D8. Uses "ad hocracy" and project teams to provide flexible frame for fluid needs and relationships.	|-----|-----|-----|-----|-----|		

Downside: Looks at each situation in a vacuum. Pushes on "x" and does not anticipate that "y" will pop out. Focuses on fragments and details, not holistic and focused on outcome. May see complexity, but does not know what to do and becomes paralyzed.

AREA SYNOPSIS

Place the number of each competency on the appropriate scale below.

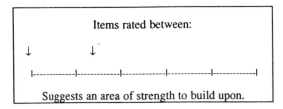

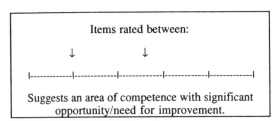

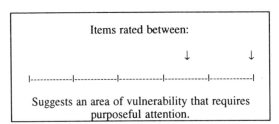

Cluster E: Deployment of Resources

Definition: Ability to prioritize and allocate time, money, materials, space, volunteer, and staff resources.

Degree of Knowledge
*(Formal Study: exposure through books
and/or courses; Experiential learning:
have successfully employed this
behavior on more than one occasion.)*

Degree of Confidence

In-Depth Knowledge	Some Knowledge	Little or No Knowledge	COMPETENCIES	Do Very Well	Get By Most of Time	Expect To Have Problems
|-----|-----|-----|-----|-----|			E1. Empowers others by communicating clear vision of outcomes desired and accountabilities; provides the authority and resources to accomplish the outcome; inspires and evaluates performance effectively.	|-----|-----|-----|-----|-----|		
|-----|-----|-----|-----|-----|			E2. Values strategic planning and links all organizational decisions to the plan.	|-----|-----|-----|-----|-----|		
|-----|-----|-----|-----|-----|			E3. Effectively uses intangible assets of the organization to create results and opportunity.	|-----|-----|-----|-----|-----|		
|-----|-----|-----|-----|-----|			E4. Clearly focuses on the long-term outcomes, letting go of the need to micro-manage or control, but rather giving others the freedom to contribute creatively.	|-----|-----|-----|-----|-----|		
|-----|-----|-----|-----|-----|			E5. Weighs priorities, (a) perceived value, (b) sequence, and (c) resource requirements when making resource decisions	|-----|-----|-----|-----|-----|		

Downside: Wasted energy and resources—much ado about nothing, i.e., lots of activity, but no result. Fragmentation of efforts.

AREA SYNOPSIS

Place the number of each competency on the appropriate scale below.

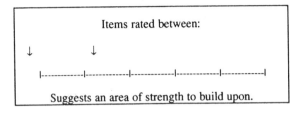

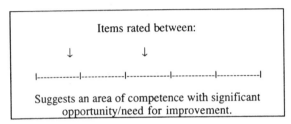

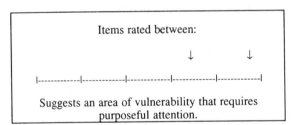

Cluster F: Personal Characteristics Common to All Clusters

Degree of Knowledge
*(Formal Study: exposure through books
and/or courses; Experiential learning:
have successfully employed this
behavior on more than one occasion.)*

Degree of Confidence

In-Depth Knowledge	Some Knowledge	Little or No Knowledge	COMPETENCIES	Do Very Well	Get By Most of Time	Expect To Have Problems
|------|------|------|------|------|			F1. Cultivation and trust of intuition.	|------|------|------|------|------|		
|------|------|------|------|------|			F2. Opportunistic—always looking for what is emerging that might be turned to advantage.	|------|------|------|------|------|		
|------|------|------|------|------|			F3. Ability to view all things holistically/multidimensionally.	|------|------|------|------|------|		
|------|------|------|------|------|			F4. Open, receptive, and relaxed (absence of fear or defensiveness.)	|------|------|------|------|------|		
|------|------|------|------|------|			F5. Respect for the interdependence of people, actions, resources....	|------|------|------|------|------|		
|------|------|------|------|------|			F6. Oriented toward providing others with the tools they need, i.e., leader as servant.	|------|------|------|------|------|		
|------|------|------|------|------|			F7. Values simplicity and clarity, and the importance of articulating what success will look like.	|------|------|------|------|------|		
|------|------|------|------|------|			F8. Ability to inspire, teach, and persuade.	|------|------|------|------|------|		
|------|------|------|------|------|			F9. Self-responsibility, self-trust, self-esteem, sociability, and integrity.	|------|------|------|------|------|		

Downside: Ego-centered: "I am right and I am important." Fear of: Change, taking risks, complexity, failure. Corrects symptoms, but not root causes.

AREA SYNOPSIS

Place the number of each competency on the appropriate scale below.

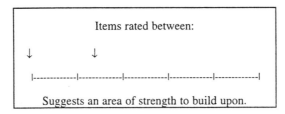

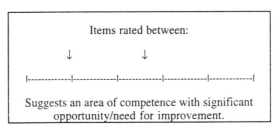

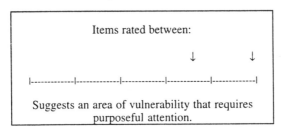

Personal Profile

↑

HIGH   —   —   —   —   —   —

	Cluster A Inter-Personal	Cluster B Tech-nology	Cluster C Infor-mation	Cluster D Relation-ships	Cluster E Resources	Cluster F Personal
6						
5						
4						
3						
2						
1						

LOW

↓

DIRECTIONS

Using both your degree of knowledge *and* degree of confidence self-ratings, locate your perceptual snapshot for each cluster on the appropriate scale-line above.

APPENDIX B
About the High-Level Organizational Scan

The organizational productivity model is a portrait of every organization, regardless of its condition. The purpose of the high-level organizational scan is to allow you (with or without partners) to develop a perceptual assessment of the relative condition of your organization.

This compressed self-study is best conducted by:

- reading the definitions of each element in the transformational clusters;
- ensuring common understanding of the definition;
- rating each element on the tabulation sheet using the rating key suggested at the top of the sheet;
- using the perceptual snapshot on the last page of the instrument to agree on a perception-based classification of the overall health of your organization.

The primary uses of the organizational scan are to:

- provide a road map for conducting an appraisal of organizational condition;
- provide a common vocabulary for group assessment of organizational condition; and

147

- provide a tool for continuous assessment and management of each element and the effectiveness of fit among them.

Many associations employ the instrument as a tool for leadership teams and outside objective expertise to identify the relative condition of each component and establish an action agenda for continuous improvement.

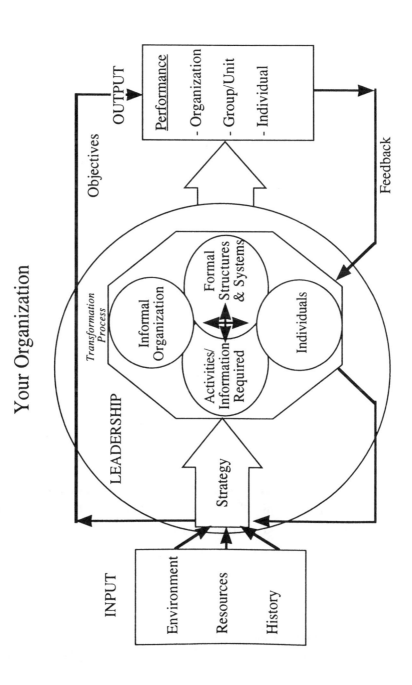

ORGANIZATIONAL PRODUCTIVITY MODEL

Your Organization

Definitions

INPUT

Environment: All factors, including institutions, groups, individual, and events outside the boundaries of the organization being analyzed but potentially influencing that organization.

Resources: Various assets that the organization has access to, including human resources, technology, capital, information, etc., as well as less tangible resources like reputation in the market.

History: The key events and patterns of past behavior, activity, and effectiveness of the organization which may have an effect on current functioning. These usually reflect and reinforce the beliefs and values held—and upheld—by the organization. These, in turn, are based upon the organization's underlying assumptions about its own internal operations and its environment.

PERFORMANCE (Output directed toward objectives)

Organizational: The measures of effectiveness of the entire system, such as whether or not it achieves its major goals, whether it makes effective use of all its resources, or whether it can adapt to changes in the environment.

Group/Unit: The effectiveness of such parts of the organization as measured by productivity and quality of the processes used to produce products, and how well units work together in achieving overall system goals; for example, how well information is exchanged between units and the degree of collaboration or conflict.

Individual: The behavior of individuals concerning the accuracy and timeliness of their work, absenteeism, punctuality, role satisfaction within the organization, etc.

FEEDBACK

Feedback: Information about the output of the organization or its components which is generally gathered through coordination and control mechanisms. It can be used to regulate the input and the transformation process.

THE ORGANIZATION (Transformation Process)

DIRECTING COMPONENTS

Strategy: The decisions made about how organizational resources will be configured to meet the demands, constraints, and opportunities presented by the environment in the context of history. In this broad sense, strategy addresses overall purpose, tactical methods and key success factors, specific actions and objectives, and the ideology needed for successful implementation.

Leadership: The directing, guiding, motivating and potentially transforming role of managers, especially those at higher levels, to create—or recreate—an organization to meet the challenges of its environment. Leaders must be able to both deeply understand and transcend their immediate organizational culture in order to fashion and communicate a clearly articulated vision of the future. This vision must at once be simple, easily understood, clearly desirable, and energizing. By empowering others and gaining commitment, often through direct participation, major changes can become institutionalized and persistent. At all stages, leadership must not only ask whether their vision is appropriate to the organization, but whether their style meets its needs.

CORE COMPONENTS

WORK

The basic set of management and non-management functions necessary to carry out the organization's strategy. The critical features of this component include:

Knowledge & Skill Requirements: The complexity of the work as measured by the education, technical understanding or specific skills necessary for its performance.

Information Processing Requirements: The amount of information that must be obtained when performing the work.

Inherent Rewards: Attributes like a sense of accomplishment, independence or social status which people may derive from performing the work.

FORMAL STRUCTURES AND SYSTEMS

STRUCTURES

The various structures, processes, methods, etc., that are formally created to aid individuals in performing tasks. They can be grouped according to structures (organizational and physical) and systems for work and for people.

Grouping: The most basic set of design decisions for structuring an organization. At the broadest level, major tasks are combined to meet the needs of the marketplace/clients and provide the competitive advantage required by the strategy. At lower, operational levels, grouping involves the design of jobs and work units, and their aggregation into larger units, divisions, departments, etc.

Linking: The set of design decisions that complements grouping by providing coordination and control mechanisms to relate separately grouped but interdependent units. Linking is as integral part of design from the organizational level down to positions within work groups. Key linking mechanisms (in order of increasing capacity to process information) are rules and procedures, planning and goal setting, vertical information systems, and lateral relations (contacts, liaison roles, temporary task forces, permanent committees, and integrator roles and departments).

Physical Environment: The location, arrangement, and physical characteristics (heating, lighting, etc.) of the facilities and immediate surroundings in which people work.

SYSTEM FOR WORK

Methods and Practices: The policies, rules, procedures and guidelines established for doing work in the organization.

Information Technology: The Electronic Data Processing (EDP) mechanisms and procedures by which information is collected and disseminated throughout an organization to perform or monitor the work process. Such information may have strategic, competitive implications by increasing efficiencies or providing significant linkages to—and benefits for—supplier and clients/users.

Support Systems: The mechanized equipment and services needed to do a job efficiently. These systems range from word processing and graphic arts services, to research libraries and intercompany mail, to voice and data communications network.

SYSTEMS FOR PEOPLE

Human Resources Management Systems: The availability, flexibility, and appropriateness of those formal systems used to select, move, appraise, and develop people, such as job evaluation plans, potential appraisal plans, training systems, etc.

Reward Systems: The flexibility, frequency, and visibility of promotion, pay or bonus plans and other formal rewards like status symbols, special awards, etc.

INFORMAL ORGANIZATION

Interpersonal Relationships: The quality of relations between and among group members, particularly regarding surfacing and dealing with disagreement. Conflict, for example, exists when one individual or group seeks to attain its own goals by interfering or frustrating the other's attempts to reach goals.

Cliques and Coalitions: Cliques are small, highly interconnected, and fairly stable groups that are part of the networks that exist within organizations. When several cliques act in concert in response to specific issues, they are called coalitions.

Informal Working Arrangements: The informal communication patterns which evolve over time and guide the way the work is done and how people relate to each other. Examples include knowing "who to call" to get tasks expedited, informal leadership roles, and unwritten standards.

Norms and Values: Norms are the formal, usually implicit, standards of behavior which the group expects and anticipates. Values are the principles, standards or qualities the group considers worthwhile or desirable. Both are integral parts of organizational culture.

INDIVIDUALS

Knowledge and Skills: The knowledge people have and the skills they exhibit in relation to the requirements of the job.

Needs and Values: What people need and value are potentially relevant to job performance. For example, people who prefer or enjoy detailed work or selling may perform these tasks better than others who may have the same general training or ability but not the interest.

Reward Expectancies: The perceptions people have about the relationship between their performance and possible outcomes or rewards.

HIGH-LEVEL ORGANIZATIONAL SCAN

Part I: Input, Performance and Direction

INPUT	RATING			Desired Condition	Current Condition	Action Required	Target Date
	Strength (+)	Competence (•)	Remediation Required (-)				
ENVIRONMENT The organization is knowledge-able about its environment and strategically positioned.							
RESOURCES The organization has access to the resources required and employs them strategically.							
HISTORY The past behavior, activity and effectiveness of the organization is used to support current and future effectiveness.							
CLIENTS The organization is knowledge-able about the wants, needs and desires of the clients it seeks to serve.							

	RATING			Desired Condition	Current Condition	Action Required	Target Date
	Strength (+)	Competence (•)	Remediation Required (-)				
PERFORMANCE							
ORGANIZATION The organization achieves quality performance and adapts easily to its changing environment.							
GROUP/UNIT The distinct parts of the organization operate in collaboration, exchange information freely and contribute to the achievement of organizational performance.							
INDIVIDUAL Individual behavior results in accuracy, timeliness, excellence and enthusiasm as behavioral norms.							
DIRECTION							
STRATEGY The organization has clearly articulated what success will look like and organizes its resources to strategically achieve these outcomes.							

LEADERSHIP	RATING			Desired Condition	Current Condition	Action Required	Target Date
	Strength (+)	Competence (•)	Remediation Required (-)				
LEADERSHIP Leadership is exercised to strategically shape organizational direction and inspire excellence in organization, group and individual performance.							

Part II: Organization

	RATING			Desired Condition	Current Condition	Action Required	Target Date
	Strength (+)	Competence (•)	Remediation Required (-)				
ACTIVITIES/INFORMATION REQUIRED							
KNOWLEDGE AND SKILLS The required knowledge, technical and other skills are available within the organization.							
INFORMATION PROCESSING The required information for quality performance is easily accessible.							
INHERENT REWARDS Individuals experience a sense of accomplishment, independence and pride.							
FORMAL STRUCTURES AND SYSTEMS							
STRUCTURES Formal structures, processes and physical environment are designed by users and support quality performance.							

	RATING			Desired Condition	Current Condition	Action Required	Target Date
	Strength (+)	Competence (•)	Remediation Required (-)				
SYSTEMS OF WORK Policies, rules, procedures and guidelines facilitate quality performance and necessary tools are available.							
SYSTEMS FOR PEOPLE Human resources management and reward systems encourage excellence and job satisfaction.							
INFORMAL ORGANIZATION **RELATIONSHIPS** Healthy and dynamic interpersonal relationships exist, promoting organizational cooperation and minimizing conflict.							
INFORMAL WORK ARRANGEMENTS The "real" work flow supports organizational goals, rather than undermining organizational effectiveness.							

	RATING			Desired Condition	Current Condition	Action Required	Target Date
	Strength (+)	Competence (•)	Remediation Required (-)				
NORMS AND VALUES Norms (standards of group behavior) and values (qualities and beliefs) exhibited within the organization are congruent with organizational goals.							
INDIVIDUALS **KNOWLEDGE AND SKILLS** Individuals possess the knowledge and skills required for success.							
NEEDS AND VALUES Individual needs and values are congruent with and not conflicting with job requirements.							
REWARD EXPECTATIONS Perceptions and expectations of individuals match performance outcomes and rewards.							

Perceptual Snapshot

[Number of "+"s]

0 1 2 3 4 5 6 7 8 **9** 10 11 12 13 14 15 16 17 **18**

Interpretation:

15 or more "+"; some "•"; no "—":	A generally healthy organization	Preserve strengths; build on competencies
9 to 15 "+"; some "•"; no "—":	A basically competent organization with unrealized potential	Preserve strengths; build up weaknesses
0 to 9 "+"; some "•"; some "—":	An organization with very significant problems	Remediate weaknesses
9 or more "—":	A generally unhealthy organization	"Fix" or dissolve